BEDS
BREAKFASTS
&
BROADCASTS

To Doris —
Happy Mother's Day, 2001
with Love from Dave
+ Best Wishes from
Carol + Bob

BEDS
BREAKFASTS
&
BROADCASTS

by

Bob & Carol Belfance

Hybrid Books
McConnelsville, Ohio

FIRST EDITION
Copyright 2000 by Bob and Carol Belfance
Library of Congress Control Number: 00-134596
International Standard Book Number 0-9705479-0-0

ATTENTION ORGANIZATIONS:
Quantity discounts are available on bulk purchases of this book for fund raising purposes.
For Information: Contact Hybrid Books, P. O. BOX 383, McConnelsville, OH 43756-0383 or call 1-800 542-7171 Fax : (740) 962-4824

For Dave Williams,
a most caring friend

DEDICATION

This book is lovingly dedicated to our parents Olive and Roy Parker and Virginia and Wilber Belfance who took the time to love and nurture us. To our friends, you know who you are, who laughed with us in the good times and helped us weather the bad times. And finally, to those special folks in our universe who create an environment of comfort and civility for their guests, the stalwart proprietors of Bed and Breakfasts throughout the world.

PREFACE

**Editors Note: Bob & Carol "talk" in different type faces
Bob** uses this type face **& Carol this type face**

This book came about because, at a dinner party given by one of our dearest friends Mary Felver, another of our dear friends, Lynette Brown said , "You guys really should write a book. The stories you could tell are fantastic."   This sort of talk definitely brings one up short, to say the least. "Write a book you say?" we said... in unison; "What about?"

Lynette, who once had a pet iguana named Petunia, smiled in her slightly feline way and then, speaking with the speed of an alien space ship in warp drive (we have often speculated about Lynette's mode of travel), ticked off: "Your lives before you bought the B&B, after you bought the B&B, a section with some of your guests' favorite recipes and another about the radio show you do from your dining room... and, of course, you'll include a CD with excerpts."

Jack Bennett/aka "Professor Jack" (we'll explain later) chimed in with "What a great idea!" and Mary rang in "Darlings you must!" Little did they know that we would take them at their word.

We left Mary's dinner party well fed and in high spirits. We were in Akron (Ohio) for the Christmas holidays visiting kith and kin, touching base with friends and enjoying that festive time of the year. As we drove to my parent's home I said, "Bob, do you think Lynette was serious about the book?"

"I don't know. What got me was how excited Mary and Jack were about the prospects of a book. Lynette is a sweetheart and I love her dearly, but sometimes she does tend to get carried away with one of her "mental flashes".

"True... but you've always said she has great instincts and that it was her instincts that made her a good actress. Perhaps we should at least give her idea some serious consideration?"

"We'll see."

"I hate it when you say 'We'll see.' If my parents said 'We'll see' when I asked for a doll or something, it always meant NO." Bob changed the subject by punching up a tape of Cole Porter tunes and we drove to my Mom and Dad's in silence. At that point I was convinced that "The Book" was a dead issue. Ha!

"It was a dark and stormy night." Now it is easy to understand why **SNOOPY** seems so at a loss as he sits at his typewriter atop his doghouse. It is all very exciting, not to mention flattering, to be at a dinner party and have someone say (very loudly) "You guys should write a book." The ego trip is fantastic. But then reality sets in.

Have you ever tried to write a book? It is not easy! What do you put in it? What do you leave out? Bob and I spent many hours talking about "The Book" and many, many more hours at the computer laboring over the key board in an effort to organize our life on paper. A Herculean task, since no one we know would ever classify our lifestyle as orderly. Rather like controlled chaos, if the truth be known.

PART ONE

JOURNEY TO THE LAND THAT MUFFLERS FORGOT

Country Boy - City Girl
Small Town USA
Facilitating Lady
Malta Maidens
Phantom Of The Opera House
The Town Crier
A Mighty Woodsman, He
Unsung Heroine
The Busy "B's"
The Queen Mum
Excelsior!

PART TWO

COOKING IS OUR LIFE

Easy Rider	Breakfast Pudding Recipe
Brian's Song	Three Cheese Puff Recipe
Two On The Aisle	Apple Crisp With A Twist Recipe
The Game's Afoot	Orange-Vanilla French Toast Recipe
Fe Fi Fo Fum	Eggs Ranchero Omelet Recipe
Have Gun, Will Travel	Scrambled Egg Toast Cups Recipe
The "Pooter" Queen	Pear Puff Pancake Recipe

PART THREE

"BREAKFAST AT THE OUTBACK"

Carol Casts Our Bread Upon The Water
Johnny III
*Professor Jack
*Cover Girl
*You Are There
*Two Broadway Babies
*A Wandering Minstrel, Aye
*A Spiced Pair
*Hobgoblins And Mayhem
*The Actress

***Excerpts from broadcasts featuring these radio guests are listed on the Compact Disc found at the back of the book.**

PART FOUR

RADIO RECIPES
&
OTHER FAVORITES

PART ONE

Journey To The Land That Mufflers Forgot

or

From Showbiz To The Outback

COUNTRY BOY - CITY GIRL

I was raised in Cranesville, New York, population 650. That's if you counted the chickens and the dogs. My dad was born on a farm surrounded by twelve brothers and sisters. An alternating half of the family "went to town" every-other Saturday to buy items not grown on the farm, such as fabric to make clothing, or visit barber shops and beauty parlors. My mom grew up in Amsterdam, New York, the eldest of three sisters, all of them "city girls". My folks probably chose Cranesville in order to live three miles from "Grandma & Grandpa in the city" and four miles from "Grandma and Grandpa on the farm". It was never mentioned, but I believe Mom and Dad chose their homestead for its geography, rather than its scenic beauty.

My Mom was born in Spencer, West Virgina, and moved to Akron, Ohio, with my Grandparents when she was seven. My Dad was born in the rural community of East Liberty, Ohio, and moved to Akron when he was five. Akron was called "The Rubber Capital of the World" in those days and many people migrated north to secure jobs in the rubber shops, building tires. When I arrived on the scene, Akron boasted two major movie theaters, The Loews and The Palace (each seating over 2,500), The Colonial theater owned by George M. Cohan which offered live plays, one burlesque theater, offering whatever burlesque theaters offered, a multitude of small neighborhood movie theaters and four radio stations.

There were also several amateur theater groups
presenting plays. Neighbors were "neighborly"
but you didn't know all that many of them and you
locked you door at night. As of this writing,
Mom's side of the family, the Eplings, have an
annual family reunion. It is a fun way to keep
track of what's happening in the family, eat some
great "down home cookin'" and enjoy swapping
much-told, favorite family stories.

Carol and I are only children whose fathers were both
union members. My dad was with the International
Brotherhood of Electrical Workers and Carol's with the
United Rubber Workers. We both had mothers who
worked away from the home at times (usually to earn
money to purchase "things for the house") but also
managed to be at home during the most important years of
our growing up. An education was highly prized by our
parents and they went out of their way to provide us with
"extras".

When I was growing up, it was common practice
that "socially prominent" boys and girls took
private lessons in elocution. These classes
were considered a must if one was to develop the
ability to speak clearly, eliminate stage fright
in the classroom and prepare one's self for
college. The cost for lessons was one dollar per
week for a thirty minute session. Bob and I were
"blue collar kids" - most assuredly not part of
the "upper crust", yet we both took elocution

lessons because our parents believed it would
mean a better life for us when we grew up.

Its was rather scary to discover how alike our parent's
values were. Carol and I took piano lessons; she had
dancing classes and I studied singing. We were never made
aware of the sacrifices our parents made to provide these
lessons but it was made clear to us that we were not
required to continue any of our "after school activities".
Needless to say, I was a-dyed-in-the-wool extrovert and
never considered giving up activities that placed me in
front of an audience and did wonders for my self-
confidence (or was it just an ego thing?). Carol, (and I find
this hard to believe) claims she was very shy until she
began to study dance. From then on her confidence grew
along with her boundless talent.

I know its love because Bob tends to go a bit
overboard when talking about me. I find it
interesting that many top level business persons
credit their success to having employed a
personal coach to help their careers along. The
coach worked at "making over" the client by
correcting bad speaking habits, instilling
confidence, improving people skills and
suggesting changes in wardrobe.   These coaches
earn fees in the thousands of dollars. How about
that?.....our parents provided Bob and me with
many of the same elements for one dollar per
week. Now when I look back at those wonderful
years of growing up I'm very grateful for all

that early training and the opportunities
afforded me by my parents...and Bob feels the
same way about his folks.

Information about our lives **B. B. I.** (before becoming
innkeepers) can be found at the back of the book.   Suffice
it to say, I started my career as a radio actor at the age of
nine, worked as an actor, production stage manager and
director in New York City, migrated to Akron, and helped
build a new community theater for the city.

After receiving my BS in Home Economics and MA in
Theatre from the University of Akron, I taught a
multitude of classes in the Speech, Theater and
Communication departments at the University. I
also taught acting at Bob's theater. Bob and I
produced and appeared in radio and television
commercials, industrial films and did "voice
overs" for a vast array of regional and national
products.

When we saw a newspaper ad for a B&B for sale in
southeastern Ohio (location unspecified) it
touched upon a subject which we had been
discussing for a while: becoming innkeepers. We
called and left a message for the owners and a
couple of days later they contacted us and
divulged the Inn's location - McConnelsville,
Ohio. Out came the map to locate this unheard of
place and arrangements were made to travel south
to have a look-see.

Could this be the answer to our prayers? Had God decided that McConnelsville was where we could make our contribution in his service?

We drove into downtown McConnelsville and immediately admired the mid-to-late-1800's buildings, including the beautiful Court House. We knew that the area looked a little seedy and rundown, but the problems seemed to be merely cosmetic, not structural. The sturdy 1870 Inn was filled with wonderful oak woodwork and good-sized rooms with private baths. We visited the nearby (4 blocks) Howard House Restaurant and were amazed by the beauty of the place and the excellence of the food. What a convenient place for guests to dine in the evening - a definite plus for a B&B.

A visit to the Opera House on the square, where movies are shown on weekends for the princely sum of $2.00, proved to be love at first sight. The magnificent acoustics and a real raked, oak stage was just icing on the proverbial cake!

On our many visits, people kept speaking to us as though they knew us. We loved the Court House clock tolling the hours as we went on our many exploratory strolls about the village. And two and a half blocks from the Inn was the Muskingum River and the hand operated lock. It is one of a series of locks that connect Roscoe Village to the Ohio River at Marietta.

In point of fact, you can launch your boat at McConnelsville and sail to Pittsburg or New Orleans!

For six weeks we spent Saturdays in Southeastern Ohio asking, listening. Driving home from what seemed our umpteenth trip, Carol leaned over and whispered, "I think this is the place we're supposed to be. Lets do it!" "OK by me," I said, and our new adventure began.

SMALL TOWN, USA

The village of McConnelsville was part of the "when this war is won" dream held by General Robert McConnel as he led his young United States Army troops during the War of 1812..

On land purchased for $1.75 per acre, the General platted his village and, in the spring of 1817, registered said plats into the County Records at Marietta. That fall, Jacob Kahler built a log cabin on his one-fifth acre lot (all lots were of this size). In 1826 the village consisted of a few dwellings scattered here and there. Ten years later, (1836) with over 105 families on its tax rolls, McConnelsville was incorporated. Today about 2,000 residents call McConnelsville home. The General provided two lots each for the Presbyterian, Methodist, Baptist and Friends Churches. He also set aside

two five-acre plots for Military Parade Grounds
... so used in the early days of the village's
history. Today these areas are known as The
Commons and The Grove.

Morgan County was formed in December of 1817 and in
1818 McConnelsville became the County Seat. At one
time the village was an important stop for riverboats using
the Muskingum River to transport goods and passengers to
Marietta and Zanesville. Later on, railroads and improved
turnpikes provided a means to quicker and cheaper
transportation and the riverboats slowly faded from the
scene.

It was not surprising to find that residents of the quaint
village of McConnelsville located in Morgan County were
very much like the folks I grew up with. This area of
southeastern Ohio known as "Ohio's Outback" includes
Morgan County. It is also part of **Appalachia**, a
geographic area that covers parts of 12 states from
northern Mississippi to southern New York State. Geo-
politically, it is defined as a mountainous, hilly area
stretching about 1,200 miles in length and 300 miles wide.
Significant portions of Pennsylvania, Maryland and Ohio
(29 of Ohio's 88 counties) lie within its geographic and
cultural boundaries. Cranesville (my hometown) is
situated about fifty miles north of Appalachia on the
Mohawk River in central New York State.

**The people of Morgan County are typical of most
Appalachian folk... friendly, helpful and**

welcoming, up to a point. If you, your parents,
grandparents, and great-grand parents were
people born and raised in the area, "yer from
'round here". Your identity is who you are. This
does not relate to your name alone, but who your
family is, where you live, what school you
attend, your church affiliation and what you
believe.

If your family is "not from 'round here" (within the county
line), then you're a G.D.O., which is short for "gol' durn
outsider". You "best hesh up" (be quiet) and "git shed of"
(get rid of) any ideas that might be new or different. Some
who live in Morgan County take pride in saying, "We bin'
doin' it like this since before I was borned and we sure as
shootin ain't a-fixin' (getting ready) to change it."

Moving to McConnelsville (called "The Land
Mufflers Forgot" by one of our guests) posed no
great difficulties for me since many of the
townspeople reminded me of the aunts, uncles,
and cousins I knew when I was a child. Living in
this environment does take some getting used to.
The rhythm and tempo of rural life is much slower
than in the cities. People tend to talk about new
ideas for about four years and then think "We've
done that, haven't we?"

The in-bred aspects of Appalachia have been well
documented by historians and anthropologists.

Bob made mention of the "closed mindedness" of Morgan Countians, but we should explain that not everyone in the county thinks this way. Slowly, ever so slowly, a shift in thinking toward improving the local economy and quality of life in Morgan County is taking hold. One example is a $1,100,000 project that will physically restore McConnelsville's Historic Downtown which encompasses an eclectic blend of architectural styles beginning in the early 1800's. Bob was Chairman of the Morgan County Chamber of Commerce's Downtown Revitalization Committee that succeeded in securing $700,000 in state and federal grant money. The balance came from local businesses, $300,000, and the Village of McConnelsville, $100,000.

When we arrived in McConnelsville the unemployment rate was 19.2%. A major furniture plant had closed, coal miners were being laid-off and, if you wanted to work, you were forced to drive as much as 90 minutes to get to an available job.

Carol was being gracious when she says that moving to McConnelsville posed no problems for her. We took possession of our B&B on **August 29, 1994**. A date that will live, not in infamy, or in anyone's memory but ours. It came to pass (Biblically speaking) that on August 1, 1994 I was selected as a full time consultant by a school board located only fifteen minutes from our home in Akron. The starting day for my contract?

Would you believe...**August 30th!** I was to spend the next year, Monday through Friday away from the Inn! I arrived in McConnelsville early evening every Friday and left for work at 5:45 am on Monday morning, Through all the madness, Carol carried on like the trouper she is. I forgot to mention..... our first night as Innkeepers, two of our three rooms were occupied by paying guests and I had to be on the job the next day!

I will freely admit that having one's husband away from a "Mom & Pop" business is, to understate the situation, extremely trying.

Bob always pooh-poohs me when I say that he is a true romantic.... but really, he is. How many men do you know who would charter a private aircraft so that we could spend our first night as Innkeepers together. Of course there were those "other people", aka/the guests, staying with us, so totally unbridled (and sometimes noisy) passion was out. Came the morn, I drove Bob to the Morgan County International Aero-Drome (our nickname for the Morgan County landing field) and he flew off into the sun in a Piper Cub. He wore a trench coat and snap brim fedora... I, a white suit with matching picture hat. (Not really!) Happily, Claude Raines and Paul Henreid did not show up for our farewells.

Our move to Morgan County has given us the opportunity

to make many new friends. This wonderfully diverse group of folks have helped make us feel welcome and added enrichment and enjoyment to our lives in a myriad of ways. They have guided us in getting to know our new community, answered our questions and, directly or indirectly, put our feet on those paths which made it possible to convert our ideas into actions and our actions into useful and lasting contributions to Southeast Ohio.

Although my first year in McConnelsville is still something of a blur, I will forever be grateful to a number of people who made us feel welcome in our new home and helped ease our transition to a new environment.

Up Eighth street a block from our B&B lives Jane Christie who took me to lunch at the wonderful Howard House Restaurant and went out of her way to "introduce me around". She also invited me to join "The Book Club".

Ruth Hart's home is a block east on Union (we're on the corner of 8th and Union). Ruth was and is always available to me and our guests to answer genealogical questions.

At the Kate Love Simpson Library, Kay Dye and Jane Brown were always cheerful and helpful. Jane is now my "Avon Lady" and Kay continues to be a fun free spirit in the community.

Less than a block away on South 8th Street, Rick

and Nancy Huck have been wonderful neighbors.
Rick or son Jason have been known to plow out our
sidewalk in heavy snows.

Don Keller, Editor of the *Morgan County Herald*,
pointed me in all the right directions and
encouraged me to join the Chamber of Commerce and
serve on the Tourism Committee.

Jerry Reed and her sister Betty White made me
feel most welcome at the Historical Society
meetings and continue to be helpful to me and our
guests in need of information.

Jim Allen and his employees at Central Market,
especially Doris Ray in the bakery, were always
smiling and helpful. It was so pleasant to find
that customer service is "alive and well" in
McConnelsville.

Gary Lawrence of the Howard House Restaurant is a
kindred theatrical spirit. A wonderful waiter,
professional in every way, our guests tell us he
treats them royally. It turns out that Gary is
also an excellent ballroom dancer. We caught his
turn at the Opera House as part of a local variety
show. He was really quite good. Bob and I like
him a lot.

FACILITATING LADY

Duke Ellington had his "Sophisticated Lady" but
I had Linda Moore Breese, my Facilitating Lady.
The Gods were obviously smiling upon us when they
sent Linda our way. Linda had worked for the
former owners. Since they didn't live on
premises, her duties at the Inn became quite
diverse over a period of time - cooking,
cleaning, confirming reservations, staying
overnight with the guests on an as-need basis.

About a year before our move to McConnelsville,
Linda became the primary care giver for her
grandson Rhett. So her life and ours were going
through some big changes at about the same time.

Our needs and hours seemed to mesh beautifully.
She no longer could spend the night with guests
but, since we live at the Inn, this wasn't a
problem. She reserved most of her mornings for
us to help clean and turn the rooms around for the
next sets of guests. Many mornings the three of
us resembled whirling dervishes as Linda
cleaned, I did baking and laundry as Bob did yard
work, maintenance and, of necessity, became
quite expert at basic potty repairs.

Linda is a person that you like the minute you
meet her. Her disposition is always sunny, open
and friendly.

I think she is the depository of many secrets,
because people instinctively know that she can
be trusted and therefore tend to confide in her.
One wonders whether this is sometimes a bit of a
burden!

A McConnelsville native, Linda has also lived
other places during her life's journey. She and
her former husband lived for a couple of years in
Las Vegas and then moved on to Los Angeles for
another two years before Linda returned to
McConnelsville by Greyhound bus, with nothing
more than the clothes on her back. She has seen
hard times, but they have not beaten her down or
soured her disposition. Her sense of humor is
infectious and being around her just plain makes
people feel better.

Without Linda, I don't know whether I would have
survived the first tough year here at the Inn: A
new place, a new business and a husband who was
only here weekends! Linda was always "on call"
to answer questions: "Where do I shop for
groceries?", handle the day-to-day chores or
even the unusual: "Linda, I've bought a rather
large patio table, umbrella and chair set which
the salesman managed to cram into my little
Renault, but I can't get the chairs out of the
back seats - could you come over and help?" On
Friday, Bob's jaw dropped in amazement when he

spied thelovely striped umbrella table and
wrought iron chairs on the patio.

Being a Morgan County girl, Linda knows many of
the relatives of our guests with past or present
"local connections". This information has often
proved to be very helpful. And long-term guests
really enjoy seeing her and swapping stories of
local people and happenings. She has been able
to answer a lot of "What ever happened to ...?"
questions over the years. But, having lived
other places, she has a much broader-than-
Morgan-County perspective on local problems or
events.

We have also had the great pleasure of watching Rhett
grow from a 3-year-old who called us Karl and Gob, to a
tall-for-his-age, handsome nine year old. "Rhett stories"
are among our favorites - when he was seven, the main
thing he wanted for Christmas was a REALLY BIG
stapler!?! He can't wait to have his own law office!

One day Carol asked Linda, "Would you be interested in
working as a para-professional at the library?" "Yes, I'd love
that," she responded. She had worked in the County
Auditor's office and would certainly be capable of handling
the job. Carol dropped a few hints, made sure Linda
applied when an opening occurred, and we put in a good
word or two in her behalf. Linda still works for us when
her schedule permits but, happily, as this book goes to
press, she is also a full time employee of the Kate Love
Simpson Library. Way to go Linda!

MALTA MAIDENS

It was late afternoon on September 30, 1994, and the former owners (husband and wife) had invited "leading social and business locals" to an open house at the Inn. "This here will get you in good with the right people and give them a chance to see what you look like," said the husband. We noticed that, along with most people, we tended to back away from the loud speech pattern of the husband. Bob mentioned once that he thought he might be partially deaf.

About halfway through this proceeding, two ladies crossed our threshold, smiling broadly and possessing great self assurance. The rather tall lady, wearing vivid red lipstick and a large hat that looked just right on her, offered me her hand. "How do you do? I'm June Martin and this is my sister Gertrude." "Welcome to Morgan County," said Gertrude. "June and I wish you the best of luck with your new business. When you've settled in, you must come visit us." "We live just across the river in Malta, in the house where both of us were born," added June. Gertrude had on a lovely print dress and both she and June were wearing exquisite jewelry that had been in the Martin family for many years. The Sisters Martin are truly a study in contrasts. Gertrude, born in 1907, tends to remind one of the Victorian era when behavior was genteel.

June was born in 1921 and has a tempo and rhythm more closely attuned to that of the "Roaring Twenties".... fast and snappy.

She is a tall, bubbly woman whom Bob often has
described as "Morgan County's answer to Carol
Channing". Both girls attended Malta Elementary
School (over 100 years old and, sadly, still in
use), McConnelsville High School and Ohio
University. Gertrude also attended Malta Normal
School prior to college. Gertrude taught at
several Ohio elementary schools and June was
Food Supervisor for the Statler Hotel Chain
prior to teaching Home Economics in Ohio high
schools. Both are members of the Daughters Of
The American Revolution.

"The Martin Girls", as they are called by many of their
friends, became the first members of our "McConnelsville
family". Carol remembers how incredibly thoughtful they
were durning the year I was commuting weekends from
Akron. Gertrude would call: "Carol, June and I are ready
to go shopping in Zanesville. Why don't you come along?"
On one trip, they had an excellent soup and salad lunch at
what June called "an old beer joint we like". I hasten to
point out that, although the "Sisters Martin" were well
know there and greeted with great fondness by both staff
and patrons, they went for the contents of the menu, not
to imbibe. It was not a place Carol would have ventured
into on her own. One can only wonder what first
prompted the Martin Sisters to give it a try.

One afternoon in November, June stopped by the
Inn. "The Morgan County Historical Society
meets tonight; the program should be pretty good

and it's a terrific way to meet people. Oh, I
almost forgot, they always have something good
to eat after the meeting, too!" The food was,
indeed, very good. Gertrude was a member of the
Board of Trustees at that time and she introduced
me in a most graceful manner. The members in
attendance were very cordial. Bob was in town
for the Christmas meeting which was held two
blocks from the Inn at the home of our neighbor,
Jerry Reed. We joined the Society that night and
about six months later Bob was elected Vice
President.

As a new and rather naive member of the Chamber of
Commerces' Tourism Committee, I volunteered to
create an historic walking tour of
McConnelsville. Being one of those odd ducks who
really enjoy researching things at the library
and also wanting to learn more of the fascinating
history of our new hometown, this seemed a
perfect project. The task seemed simple enough
until I started digging into the library
material. I had little to go on and called
Gertrude for advice. I explained the project to
her, what I needed to put the tour together and
gave her a copy of my working notes. "June and I
will drive you around town and fill you in on the
oldest and most important buildings in the
village if you like," she said cheerfully.
To gather the material I needed, it took one

afternoon of touring the town. With the effervescent June at the wheel and Gertrude pointing the way, we had a joyous afternoon.

Bob edited my copy and secured art work for the project. Finally, Chamber of Commerce member Jim Kelly, Sprint's Community Development Manager, graciously provided the printing and the paper stock for the brochure and the walking tour became a reality. Visitors and locals alike seem to enjoy it.

Between them, there is very little history of the area that the Martins aren't aware of or actually remember. Gertrude, age six, lived through the 1913 flood. It was the worst in the Muskingum Valley's history and her memories are still quite vivid. "My father, who managed a mantle manufacturing plant located close to the river, came home to tell us that the river was rising fast. That night my Dad's plant and the canning plant next door were torn from their foundations by the raging waters. When both buildings hit and took out the metal bridge, down-river, it sounded like a enormous explosion! I'll never forget those sounds coming out of the darkness. Several days later we learned that every bridge between Zanesville and Marietta had been swept away."

Even though their careers took them to other states or different locations, their collective memories of growing up along the Muskingum River remain fresh and detailed. They have a mental storehouse of who's related to whom (and how) and what happened when.

River town children grow up with rich, varied and sometimes scary experiences. A river can be calm and tranquil or uncontrolled and numbingly frightening. But we love to imagine a very young Gertrude, with baby June in tow, ice skating with her friends on the Muskingum's frozen surface.

PHANTOM OF THE OPERA HOUSE

Located on our Village Square is the crown jewel of downtown McConnelsville, the Opera House. It was built by our village fathers and is still owned by the Village. Originally conceived of as a Town Hall and Opera House by architect H. C. Lindsay, the Opera House is a brilliant example of Victorian architecture at its best. It sits on the site of the Brewster Hotel which had burned to the ground. Construction was begun in 1890 and on May 28, 1892 the Opera House offered a production of Gilbert and Sullivan's **The Mikado**.

Newspaper articles of events leading up to the opening night performance reported that the Opera House would be the first building in Morgan County to be wired for electricity. As word spread that the "new light of day" would be used to illuminate the stage production, ticket sales skyrocketed. On opening night 800 southeastern Ohioans filled the opera house to capacity. They had traveled by railroad, riverboat, horse and buggy, and "shank's mare" to witness the performance. And for a while they did ... until the lights failed. In the best tradition of the theatre, "the show must go on" and in short order candles were secured, the actors went back to the opening scene of the operetta and, when the curtain call concluded, all went home happy and entertained.

For the people of Morgan County, the Opera House was the center of community life. It was the "home" for melodramas, minstrel shows and medicine shows.

Touring theatrical companies presented plays by Shakespeare and the many popular musicals of that era. Billy Sunday preached from the stage, McDonald Birch, a star attraction on international stages, presented countless magic shows there. Vaudeville performances, always a crowd-pleaser, flourished until talking pictures took their place. This meant fewer live shows at the Opera House and in 1936 the Opera House became a full-fledged, 600 seat movie theatre, complete with the most modern equipment available at that time. By 1962 the opera house was in disrepair, audiences were dwindling, and the future looked bleak for the "Grand Old Lady On The Square". It was at this point that Galen Finley, once an usher and at that time an assistant to the owner, stepped

forward and purchased the contents of the Opera House.
"I couldn't bear to see it close," he said.

When we purchased our B&B, we found a number of
Victorian-style, hand-held fans celebrating the
Opera Houses' one hundredth anniversary. A
history of the Opera House was printed on their
back sides and touched on Galen's purchase of the
Opera House. Several months later, Bob and I met
Galen Finley at the annual Christmas Meeting of
the Morgan County Historical Society. He turned
out to be a charming man with a passion for the
Opera House, McConnelsville, and Morgan County.

"Did you really live on the stage of the Opera
House, behind the movie screen?", I asked him.

"Oh yes, I spent all the money I had to buy the
Opera House so I had to live there, too. It was
actually quite comfortable because of the
hundreds of antiques my grandmother helped me
collect, starting when I was seven years old.
She used to send me to the town dump when she
heard that someone was getting rid of an old
table or desk and I brought it home in my little
red wagon. I had quite a collection of stuff
before I was twenty. My living area was as fancy
as the Opera House. I used tapestries and drapes
to create living spaces. I had a working
fountain, marble top tables, poofs, Grecian
urns, cut crystal and when I was finished it

looked like a sheik's harem. I had a really
elegant casket one Halloween."

In 1968 the Mayor and Village Council wanted to
close the Opera House and convert it to office
space. "I was horrified to think that our
Village would loose one of its most valuable
assets, so I ran for Mayor. I had only one plank
in my platform, 'Save The Opera House!', and I
won."

The Opera House is run by a non-profit
organization now. It presents mostly movies
with an occasional "live" presentation. Sadly,
very few plays are to be seen on its hallowed
"boards".   A plaque honoring Galen is to be found
in the lobby.

Galen Finley and The Opera House are often spoken
of in the same breath and with good cause. Many
people spend their lives saying, "I wish I had
..... I wish I had!" Not Galen Finley! He can
proudly say , "I'm glad I did! -I'm glad I did!"

THE TOWN CRIER

Every Wednesday morning I walk up-town, all two blocks,
to purchase a copy of the **Morgan County Herald**. After
scanning the first page I always turn to page two, upper left
hand corner, to see what Sara Hurst is writing about in her

column, **Side Salad.** You can always count on Sara to either enlighten or entertain you. Her style is clear and precise and, as they say in the newspaper business, "an easy read". You can always relate to what she's writing about.

I was introduced to Sara at the Herald offices by the aforementioned former owner. "Be nice to her, she can do you some good," he hissed as we approached Sara's desk. "Welcome to Morgan County and good luck in your new venture," she said as she offered me a big smile and a firm handshake. You don't have to work at finding ways to like Sara; she's a jolly and caring lady with a sweetly devilish sense of humor.

Sara has been at the Herald for twenty one years, as Assistant Editor since 1988, and for twenty years was the area correspondent for the Zanesville Times Recorder. She has written numerous articles for Around Ohio Magazine.

Carol introduced me to Sara at an Historical Society meeting. We have become fast friends and email buddies. Her sunny disposition and dry humor have often saved the day when a meeting started to get a little testy.

I am amazed at her ability to accomplish so much for so many. In addition to her column, Sara covers newsworthy events, edits news, and is secretary for at least four service organizations. I asked her one day if she had a favorite moment as a reporter. Her response was lightning quick. "I had the opportunity to do a one-on-one interview with

the late President Richard M. Nixon. It was quite a thrill!
I had met senators and congressmen, but never the
President of the United States."

**Sara and her husband Lou have raised three sons
(all graduates of Ohio State University) who
have produced four grandchildren - all of whom
they spoil when given the opportunity. She has
given unselfishly of her time and talents to help
make Morgan County a better place for everyone.
Her civic contributions include the Chamber of
Commerce, where she has been secretary for more
years than she cares to remember. The Historical
Society, Genealogical Society, Morgan County
Emergency Planning Committee have also been
beneficiaries of her volunteer efforts. Sara
also served a seven-year stint on the Board of
Trustees of Washington State Community College
during its growth years, taught Sunday School
for 25 years and still finds time to voluntarily
help all the out-of-town people who call her at
the Herald for historical or genealogical
information.**

In 1999, Sara received the Ohio Community Citizen
Award from the Ohio State Grange in recognition for her
many contributions to the community. There can be no
doubt in anyone's mind that Sara deserved the award.
When I told Carol about Sara's award she remarked,
"What took them so long?"

A MIGHTY WOODSMAN, HE

One morning in January of 1996 I received a call from a delightful young woman (Wendy Jo Ray) employed by the American Electric Power Company asking about current room availabilities. We booked a room for a Mr. Gary Kaster. Little did I know that over the next several years he would play an important part in Carol's and my life.

Gary turned out to be a soft spoken man with a quizzical smile and a dry sense of humor. He was being transferred back to Morgan County and would need a room, usually Monday thru Thursday, thereby eliminating a 90 minute drive to and from his office. Gary stayed with us for parts of three weeks until, finally, he and his wife Susan were able to set up temporary housekeeping in the county. Gary and Susan had lived in Morgan County for twenty years when Gary was abruptly transferred to AEP'S Columbus office. Two years later, after they had sold their home, back they came. Susan and Gary eventually built a lovely new home here in the county. One can only hope that another transfer is not in their future.

Gary asked for breakfast at 6:00 am because "I like to be at the office no later than seven." Over the course of his stays I think he left for work at close to eight o'clock. Carol and I were anxious to know as much about Morgan County as possible and Gary was willing to share his knowledge with us. We talked about the school system, local economy, unemployment, and what was needed to help "bring back" the county.

I was surprised to learn that coal mining is not the only ancillary business with which AEP is connected.

Born and raised in Canton, Ohio, Gary is AEP's Forestry and Recreation Programs Supervisor. This means he's responsible for all forest management, reforestation and recreation on AEP lands throughout seven states. One of the programs that Gary spearheaded was AEP'S planting of 15 million trees by the year 2000 as part of a worldwide commitment to put more oxygen back into our atmosphere.

The other area of Gary's work, which seems like a fun part of his job, relates to what is called ReCreation Land. This is an area of over 49,000 acres of reclaimed coal fields which are located eight miles northeast of McConnelsville. Available, free to the public, visitors can take part in camping, fishing, hunting, hiking, horseback riding or just enjoying the outdoors. I have never asked Gary what aspect of his job he enjoys the most but, when he talks about ReCreation Land, it is patently obvious that he takes great pride in his accomplishments there. The fact that over 100,000 people use this area each year is, I know, very gratifying for him.

Gary is always anxious to help with any project. In the late summer of 1996 I asked if AEP would be willing to donate a forty-foot-tall, fresh cut Christmas Tree to be placed on The Commons as part of the annual Festival Of Lights.

"I thought that we just had decorated store windows and hanging snow flakes on the lamp posts. Is this something new?" I then explained that I had suggested a Community Tree and short program to include: Christmas Carols, Carol reading "'Twas The Night Before Christmas", me reading "Yes Virginia, There Is A Santa Claus" and, finally, the lighting of the tree. All this preceded by a parade with lighted floats! Gary said yes, and later supplied me with photos of six trees to choose from, and delivered and erected the tree. Larraine Hunt of the Morgan County Metropolitan Housing Authority provided the funds for lights and over 600 people attended the first program. The Community Tree Lighting is now an annual event that has grown in popularity each season.

Bob spent three exciting years as a member of the Board of Directors of the Chamber of Commerce and, when asked, he agreed to Chair their Downtown Revitalization Committee. Because McConnelsville's entire Historic Downtown is on the National Register of Historic Buildings. The goal of the project was to take the area back to the former 1800's river town it had been by bringing back all the elements of the late 1890's. This meant changing signage, installing turn-of-the-century light posts and a myriad number of period components. He and the committee were charged with designing the project, seeking grants, and eliciting the support of the business community for the project. As part of the project, Bob asked Gary

if AEP would supply 30 trees to be used to
beautify the downtown. "You got 'em." said Gary,
"It's a great project and AEP is 100% behind it."
As of this writing, the trees are in the ground, a
one million, one hundred thousand dollar
Downtown Revitalization project is under way
and, not surprisingly, Gary is ably serving on
the Board of Directors of the Chamber.

UNSUNG HEROINE

Some people in Morgan County might say that Della Belle
Murphy Bratton's "bite" is worse than her "bark". I know
her to be a loving and caring wife, mother, doting
grandmother, and a woman of courage and conviction.

She is one of five children born to James Henry and Flora
Mae Parker Murphy (her sister Mary Leeck Williams was
adopted).   Della says of her childhood, " We were taught
at an early age to work hard, be honest, respectful, patriotic
and God Fearing. On Sunday mornings and afternoons we
went to a little country church at Hopewell and were back
at McConnelsville for Sunday evening worship. Boy, was I
God Fearing."

Della takes great pride in her heritage. She enjoys telling
stories about her Great-Great-Grandfather Warner. "He
was a shoe cobbler by trade and one day, at age 76, he
decided to visit relatives in the states east of Ohio. Well,
he filled a wheel barrow with his cobbling supplies and

walked from here to Washington DC. (400 miles) He
stopped off to visit, cobbled shoes to earn some money,
and then moved on. There was a big story in the *New York
Times* about his having tea with President William Henry
Harrison at the White House. I would liked to have know
him, he seems like quite a fellow."

It was not for several years that Bob and I had
the pleasure of meeting Della .

We had read her many Letters To The Editor of the
Morgan County Herald concerning local social and
political issues. At times, Della's letters
tended to be so passionate that the central issue
was somewhat lost in her emotional outcry.
To be brutally frank, Bob and I avoided meeting
Della because many people were saying to us,
"she's wacky", "she should mind her own damn
business", "she's a rabble rouser". Then one
Wednesday I read to Bob a letter Della had
written to the paper about pollution problems in
the old landfill. On the spot, Bob and I decided
that this lady simply wanted assurances that
someone would look into the matter and do his
job, and we made it a point to meet Della.

We learned that Della had worked her way up from
waiting tables to Law Enforcement Secretary for the State
of Ohio's Department of Natural Resources (25 years) and

was well versed in researching the Ohio Revised Code. We also came to understand why she would "take to task" any public official who neglected to do his job.

After she retired, "I got involved with county affairs. I was appalled at conditions; roads were poor, schools were in decay, unemployment high, and planning was a joke. I set out originally to educate the people in my county regarding the need for better accountability of public funds, clearer policy procedures and the need for each public employee to do his or her job to their ability.

What I found in some cases was fraud and deception."

Della is responsible for positive changes in the Child Enforcement Agency, Election Board and the misuse of "rainy day funds". Her fight to rid the landfill of hazardous wastes is being won. Della's hard work uncovered fraud in the now defunct Home Health Care Agency. Two employees were tried, found guilty and sentenced for their criminal activities.

Remember those folks who told us "she's wacky", "she should mind her own damn business", "she's a rabble rouser"? Today they will tell you that, "Della's OK", "She knows what she's talking about", "You can trust ol' Della!" We're so glad that we were around to see the people of Morgan County recognize Della for the dedicated Fighter For Right that she truly is.

THE BUSY B'S

I think it was in September of 1995 that I was in the checkout line at Central Market when a total stranger paid her bill and said as she left, "I stopped into your shop yesterday; your husband did a beautiful job of repairing my antique pin." This seemed most strange, since we have never owned a shop and Bob was still a consultant in Akron at that time.

That weekend, Bob walked into the kitchen; he was grinning like a Cheshire cat. "Carol, I didn't know you were producing painted T-shirts on the side!" I gave him a look somewhere between quizzical and snotty but, before I could offer a retort, he was saying, "I've figured out what's going on. People think I'm Bob de la Mora, you're Brenda de la Mora and vice versa." I stopped mixing muffin batter and paused to ponder this piece of news. "Of course", I said, "that has to be it!" At the next Chamber meeting I asked Bob de la Mora if anyone had mistaken Brenda or him for us. He laughed loudly and said, "It happens just about every day. Apparently the village can't handle two guys named Bob - both with red-haired wives - moving to the area within a year of each other without causing a lot of major confusion."

The confusion continues to this day. We've even received each other's mail! We once considered

asking Sara Hurst to run a photo of "The Bobs",
plus Brenda and Carol, in the *MORGAN COUNTY
HERALD*; but then, a nightmarish thought occurred
to us: What if they captioned it wrong? People
would never get us straight!

Bob was born in San Antonio, Texas, but was raised in
both the U. S. and Mexico. At age 13 he was apprenticed
to a watchmaker and goldsmith and at ages 15, 16, and 17
he placed second in the National Arts Scholastic Program.
"Designing jewelry is my love," he says.

Brenda is a computer whiz and, early on, worked for the
FBI. Her last major governmental job, before taking early
retirement, was the design of a graphics package which was
presented to President Bush for use at the White House
and by eight federal agencies. Her real love is art. She is a
talented painter, calligrapher, designer, and crafts teacher.
In Brenda's capable and talented hands, attractive bits and
pieces become magical finished products.

The de la Moras operate THE VILLAGE CHARM on
Main Street, about two blocks from our B&B. You will
find an eclectic and exciting mix there: antiques; Brenda's
beautiful hand-painted note cards; custom-made
invitations; a variety of dresses, vests, and T shirts with
Brenda's hand-painted designs and a mix of antique jewelry
and watches, plus a superb collection of jewelry designed
and lovingly made by Bob. We frequently send friends and
relatives "Brenda" cards. Without fail, the recipients call to
tell us that they've framed them!

Keep in mind that Brenda and Bob came to Morgan
County to retire! <u>That</u> certainly didn't last
long. This couple has too much talent and energy
to "retire". We call Brenda and Bob the Busy B's
because they are involved with what seems a
myriad of activities.

Bob is Past President of the Chamber of Commerce
and currently is on it's Board, a member of the
Downtown Revitalization Committee, The Howard
Chandler Christy Art Guild, Historical Society
(as is Brenda) and both are also part of a group
of investors who created Morgan Net Plus, a
sorely needed Internet Service Provider.

Brenda has devoted her energies to working with
the children of Morgan County in the areas of art
and recreation. She continues to volunteer her
time and talents to teach in the Children's Arts
Program each summer and in an after-school
program in the public schools. Brenda recently
received a Community Service Award for her
activities in these areas. She and Bob are also
charter members of Riverside Artists, an Artists
Co-Op venture located in Marietta, Ohio.

Creative, caring, willing to give of their time and talents for
the good of others; just what you hope for in your
community. The world would certainly be a far nicer place
if more people "retired" in the same manner as Bob and
Brenda.

THE QUEEN MUM

When speaking with Gloria Meranda, one almost hears the heroic strains of **_RULE BRITANNIA_** in the background. Esperanza Staley, the very talented lady who's illustration graces the cover of our book, has her personal nick-name for Gloria... The Queen Mum.

Each spring the Chamber of Commerce sponsors a Business Fair designed to showcase our local businesses and generate sales leads. Bob and I had set up our booth and were walking about the other booths in the gym of the nearby elementary school when we came upon a very business-like lady arranging samples of her beautifully painted and glazed tiles. She was featuring herbs and vegetables that were perfect for use in upscale kitchens. We stopped to say hello and were greeted with the sound of a British lass saying, "Hello, so nice of you to pop by my booth." I looked sideways at Bob; he had a big grin on his face. I knew we were in the presence of a kindred spirit.

At that time, I was searching for artists to teach a variety of fine arts to about 70 children. Larraine Hunt, Director of the Metropolitan Housing Authority was anxious to have a summer program for her young people. I described the "Camp Of The Arts" program I had implemented for the Akron Jewish Community Center and soon the County-wide, summer Children's Arts Program (CAP) for children ages 7 - 12 was a reality. I explained the project to Gloria. Her response, "What a glorious idea, you can count on me."

And count on Gloria you can - whether it's giving generously of her time and talents or just stopping to swap a humorous story or two. We love to repeat her story (with appropriate British accent, of course) of growing up in India and attending St. Helen's Convent, a rather exclusive school run by German nuns who spoke the King's English with a heavy German accent. Several of her classmates were the children of Nepal's royal family. One immediately conjures up images of many royal tiny tots traipsing about wearing bejeweled turbans. Gloria's family moved back to England when she was 13 (her first time in her mother country). "The Brits weren't terribly welcoming when we settled in," she recalls. "You see, although I had attended that fancy private school, I spoke with the most awful German accent which I'd acquired from those Teutonic tutors. You know, people weren't in the least bit welcoming. They tended to glower a bit and give us the cold shoulder. Understandably, their memories of World War II were still strong and they couldn't really help it. Eventually I began to sound like the British citizen I am and their attitudes toward me became much more civil."

Gloria's background in the arts is wonderfully diverse. She received her formal training at Harrow College of Art and Design. As she raised her family, she worked in art-related fields with companies, providing graphic arts services, and clothing and fabric design. In their behalf, Gloria traveled to many European countries as well as Australia and India.

In 1988 she married Ohio native, Charles Meranda (her second marriage), a Senior Petty Officer with the United States Navy. In 1989 Charles and Gloria were transferred from Washington, D. C. to a naval base in Rota, Spain. Located only an hour away were several of Spain's great museums. Living off base allowed Gloria to enjoy her new environment and "soak up" the sun, the sea and the art. "I couldn't know then," Gloria recalls, "but our move to Spain was to have a profound impact on my work as an artist.

Gloria was employed at the naval base as Manager of the Arts and Crafts Department. Here she came into contact with Spanish tile artists. "I was intrigued with the possibility of adapting my work with water colors to tile art, so I worked a trade. I taught my customers drawing and they taught me how to mix my pigments and to vary the firing temperatures in my kiln in order to achieve various effects. It was a very exciting time in my artistic life."

Today, Gloria's work has won numerous awards at area art shows and her custom design and painting of tiles for use in kitchens, fireplaces, powder rooms and mantels has caught the eye of several regional interior design firms.

When Bob saw the beautiful tiles Gloria's students in the Children's Arts Program had made, he was ecstatic. "Carol, I can use these tiles as background for the opening and closing titles of our CAP video." The staff of teenage counselors had videotaped all sessions and Bob was about to produce a video about CAP that was eventually presented to local sponsors and to the library.

As the editing of the video neared completion, Bob brought the tiles home to choose those to be used for the title section. About 10 minutes into his viewing he called out, "Carol, you've got to see this." He showed me a tile that instantly called to mind Vincent van Gogh's painting, THE CROWS. Bob dialed Gloria to learn more about the work. "Yes, it's quite good and the nine-year-old girl who painted that tile is mildly brain damaged and has some difficulty with oral communication. I think she shows great potential."

Over the past several years we have come to know Gloria and Charles very well. We feel blessed to have then as trusted friends.

"EXCELSIOR!"

This is my one chance to demonstrate my erudition by calling to your attention that excelsior is from the Latin... meaning, always upward! I know this to be true because I studied Latin for four arduous years in high school. Also, it is the motto of New York State from whence I migrated.

Morgan County might consider adopting the Civil Rights Marching Song "We Shall Over Come!" as its motto. It is just now that the county is beginning to overcome the many years the area was overlooked by politicians on the state and national level. In the past, local politicians were quick to use this as an excuse: "We just don't have enough votes to get their attention." When asked what approaches they were taking with the "powers that be", their standard response was, "Why bother, it's just a waste of time."

Fortunately, a number of our hard-working business and professional leaders have been willing to work, as volunteers, to provide the leadership necessary to make "good things happen" in Morgan County. Citizens deserving recognition include Attorney John Wells (originally from Gurnsey County), Rod Gallagher(raised & educated in West Virginia), President of the First National Bank of McConnelsville, and Mike Vynalek, President of Citizens National Bank, originally from the Greater Cleveland, Ohio, area. Between them,

they are responsible for major steps forward in the areas of Downtown Revitalization, Economic Development and Education. Mike has recently become a member of the McConnelsville Village Council and we anticipate that his excellent organizational and leadership skills will be a valuable asset to the Village.

The "cherry on the sundae", to coin a phrase, was popped in place due to the efforts of the Morgan Local Schools District Superintendent, Herb Young. As this is written, three new elementary schools and a new junior high, all state-of-the-art, are under construction. Herb came into the County, saw the schools literally crumbling and said, "We must and will have new schools for our children." And he immediately set about making it happen!

In what seemed like no time at all, the State of Ohio allocated almost 20 million dollars for the new schools. Our local school district was then required to supply $8 million as its share of construction costs. A bond issue was placed on the ballot and an unbelievable 79% of the voters said "yes" to the issue. We were ecstatic!

Carol and I take great pride in the fact that we broadcast a total of 15 shows about the bond issue. We made no bones about it, we supported the issue and said so loud and often. We wanted our listeners to know all the reasons

these schools were so desperately needed and we
interviewed everyone pertinent to the situation, including

the Superintendent, school board members and the chief of
building maintenance.
We received a very nice letter from Herb Young regarding
our shows: ". . .It goes without saying that 'Breakfast at the
Outback' was instrumental in assisting the school district
with the passage of our bond issue. The radio program
provided an opportunity to put the facts before the
community. More importantly, it provided an opportunity
to dispel many rumors that normally accompany such an
election."

**We had prayed to be sent somewhere that we might
be of service. We felt that Morgan County was
that place, and set about trying to contribute
what we could with an almost missionary-like
zeal. If we have helped make things better for
the citizens of southeast Ohio, we are happy
about that. Morgan County appears to be on the
upswing and, hopefully, there are more things
for us to do and accomplish in this lifetime.**

PART TWO
Cooking Is Our Life
or

The Care And Feeding of Guests

EASY RIDER

One day, soon after we purchased the Inn, the
former owner, hereafter known as Chuckles,
loudly and rapidly proclaimed, " You got
guaranteed business ya' know, from a motorcycle
guy from Pittsburgh. That plastic bag with the
socks and underwear and stuff in the closet is
his. Name's Larry; sometimes we let him sleep on
the floor upstairs." This piece of information
elicited a look from me that probably spoke
volumes... mostly unprintable. My mind conjured
up visions of leather jackets, earth-shaking
"Harleys", tattoos and empty beer cans. But I
was able, after a lengthy pause, to say, "Hmm,
sounds interesting". My memory is fuzzy as to
what happened next. I recall that Chuckles,
after this announcement, was soon out the door.
It was his habit to frequently pop in unannounced
and gleefully recall something he had
"forgotten" to mention.

The perfect set up for disaster you say?... WRONG! It
turns out that Larry, "the motorcycle guy from Pittsburgh"
is Lawrence Grodsky, a national leader in promoting the
safe operation of motorcycles. Larry has trained over
4,000 riders since 1980 and his incisive column, "Stayin'
Safe", has been a mainstay in *RIDER MAGAZINE* since
1988. We can also report that, having observed Larry in
summer wear (ie. Bermuda shorts and T shirt), zero tattoos
have been observed.

Following is a story about what brings Larry to The Outback, excerpted and edited from our local newspaper, *The Morgan County Herald.*

"Most Morgan County residents probably do not know that Lawrence Grodsky, whose column 'Stayin' Safe", is featured monthly in *RIDER MAGAZINE,* has been using the highways and byways of Morgan County to teach his class in Neo-Alpine Touring. The class was conceived for persons planning to tour Europe on their motorcycles where higher speeds and twisty mountain roads provide the ultimate sport-touring challenge.

"The tour consists of two full days of training, riding and fun. The riders join up in Pittsburg and after an in-depth briefing on procedures they see a little of Pennsylvania, West Virginia and a great deal of Southern Ohio.

"Air Force Major K.S. Carey recounted his experiences and had this to say: 'At 6:30 in the evening we found ourselves in front of The Outback Inn, a bed and breakfast operated by Bob and Carol Belfance, a husband and wife show biz team, whose voices you might recognize. Our rooms were first rate and there was off street parking for our bikes. After dinner we toured the area on foot, resting in the relaxing pace of small town America. Local folks went out of their way to make us feel welcome.

"We were given a private tour of the Opera House
(1890). It's one of those beautiful Old World
style theatres with chandeliers, a balcony, deep
purple velvet curtains, and lots of rich wood.
We even ventured into the basement which was once
a sanctuary for escaped slaves on the
Underground Railroad.

"'Next morning, after a delicious breakfast of
fresh fruit, juices, homemade muffins, and a
generous portion of Carol's cheese puff (ed.
note, for recipe see Brian's Song page 60), we
relaxed in the living room, watched a motorcycle
video, and discussed technical aspects of
riding. Soon we were back on the wonderfully
twisty asphalt of Morgan County where we took
turns leading the group and chasing each other
around the twists and turns. It was great fun.

'"One of my fellow riders was Jon Burnett, a
morning anchor for KDKA television in
Pittsburgh, who summed up his experience saying:
'Hard to beat ... some of the best roads I've ever
driven... sound instruction and great food and
hospitality at The Outback.' "

Over the past several years we have come to look forward
to welcoming Larry and his "bikers" to the Inn. We have
met a wonderfully interesting assortment of motorcycle
enthusiasts and only one Harley (lots of BMWs and
Ducattis).

It was because of one of his students that Carol developed one of our very healthful and popular breakfast dishes.

On May 20, 1995, Larry's group included Dr. James Duggan, an Ob. Gyn. from Monroeville, Pennsylvania, near Pittsburgh. Bob and I recalled him as a nice guy with an above average sense of humor and a good appetite. Just a little over a year later, Larry was scheduled for one of his tours. He called one morning about 2 weeks before his expected arrival and asked me if I remembered Jim Duggan. I paused, braced myself for bad news and said, " Yes". Thankfully, my fears were unfounded. Larry was calling to say that the good doctor had recently had angioplasty on his heart, felt good, was scheduled for the tour and could I have skim milk and some of our Amish low fat cereal available for his breakfast. No big deal; naturola cereal is always on hand in our kitchen; it's something that Bob and I both enjoy. That was easy (or so I thought).

Not ten minutes had passed when the phone rang again. I heard a small, sad voice say, " I don't want cereal for breakfast." It took only a moment to realize that Dr. D. was on the phone: "I want to have a real meal with the rest of the guys." "Well, what can you eat," I asked, figuring that the list would be short and definitive.

"Anything that is low in cholesterol and fat,"
came the reply.... (pause) "Don't you worry;
I'll find you something good," said I. "You just
concentrate on getting here safe and sound."
"See you soon", he said, and hung up seemingly
happy and assured that a yummy, healthful
breakfast would await his taste buds.

Bob was away working on his Children's Arts
Program that morning so, for the time being, I
was on my own to come up with a tasty, healthful,
breakfast main dish for Dr. Duggan. Most people
think that, just because a recipe is
"healthful", it must taste awful. In some cases
I have found this to be true. Bob and I tried a
low fat ice cream once that tasted like cold,
vanilla-flavored grit. Such could not be the
case for dear Doctor Duggan. So the search
began.

Bob came home that afternoon to find stacks of
recipe files and cookbooks strewn about our
dining room table. "I'm looking for a recipe," I
said; "I'd have never guessed" he said with that
pseudo-naive little smile of his that at once
irritates me and reminds me of why I love him.
And then he added; "I take it the search is to be
quite extensive." A funny line? Yes. Coolly I
replied, "Are we going to do one liners all
afternoon or are we going to be a helpmate?"

He crossed to where I sat and kissed me lightly
on the cheek: " How may I be of service, madam?"
This was said in a tone that implied total
servitude...Hah!... but I knew better.

I filled him in on the "exposition" of the
situation and the search now proceeded at a
furious pace.

It is important to understand two things; we
never serve our guests anything that we have not
taste tested personally and we both felt the
ideal recipe should be palatable for Larry's
entire group.   Given the fact that Dr. Duggan
would be at our table in slightly less than two
weeks, we spent the next three hours checking my
files and reading like mad. Finally, we decided
to take a break for food and drink (homemade
turkey rice soup, salad, fresh baked cottage
cheese dill bread and lemonade). Bob looked at
me across his bowl of soup and said, "Too bad we
can't just serve them something simple like
french toast." I grunted in the affirmative and
buttered my bread.

Perhaps it was the act of buttering my bread; in
any event, my mind suddenly took me back to the
dining room of the Hotel Russell in London. In
1974 my son Jason and I had stayed there while on
a London theatre tour. The breakfasts we enjoyed
there were fabulous.

In my life to date, I have never tasted butter or
cream so fresh. I also was remembering a dish
similar to french toast called breakfast
pudding that consisted of a fairly thick slice of
bread that I thought had been soaked in a mixture
of eggs and milk and baked.

In a way it reminded me of my Grandma Vineyard's
bread pudding, except it was served on a plate
with a sprinkling of powdered sugar and a rasher
of bacon on the side. If I could concoct a proper
recipe of my own, the problem would be solved.
"Bob!", I shouted, " We'll serve Dr. Duggan
English Breakfast Pudding and add rashers of
bacon for the rest of the group!" "Great!, lets
see the recipe," he enthused. "There isn't one,"
I said. "I'll have to make one up." Bob, God
love him, nodded his head, smiled and said, " I'm
sure 'twill be a most sumptuous repast madam,
fit for all to consume." (What can I say; our
theatre background sometimes causes us to speak
somewhat oddly, with accents ranging from
British to Wolf Man.)

I was very lucky and got it right on my first
attempt. Following is my recipe for Carol's
Baked English Breakfast Pudding which Dr. Duggan
(and his fellow cyclists) loved and has become
popular with many of our guests. Enjoy!

CAROL'S BAKED ENGLISH PUDDING

1 loaf unsliced raisin bread
1 quart skim milk
8 oz. liquid egg substitute
1 Tablespoon vanilla
4 egg whites
1 teaspoon cinnamon
1/2 cup sugar
1/2 teaspoon nutmeg
2 Tablespoons corn-oil margarine, melted
powdered sugar

Grease two 8" square baking pans. Trim and discard ends from bread & slice into 8 equal slices. Arrange 4 slices on bottom of each baking pan.

In large bowl, whisk together egg substitute, egg whites. Add sugar, milk, vanilla, cinnamon & nutmeg. Mix well. Pour evenly over bread, cover pans, and refrigerate overnight.

In the morning, preheat oven to 350°. Drizzle the melted margarine over the bread & bake uncovered for 45 minutes.

When ready: Dust with powdered sugar and serve. (serves 8)

BRIAN'S SONG

Brian Carling is a jolly geologist from Chadds Ford, Pennsylvania, who holds the record for having stayed at the Inn more than any other guest (his first night with us was April 14,1996). As with most guests, our first

contact was over the phone. "Hi, this is Brian
Carling of Advanced GeoServices. I'll be
staying at your place for about a month." I had
time to say something like "Oh, how nice." "You
were recommended by one of your County
Commissioners. He said you have great
breakfasts and you're located about three
minutes from my job site" (a potentially
polluted landfill in an old sand quarry).

Brian is an energetic talker, but I did manage to
squeeze a question into the conversation. "What
dates do you have in mind?" "It looks like I'll
need three rooms for about 5 days and then just
one room for three, possibly four more weeks."
"And this would be when?" I asked. A short
pause, and then, "Didn't I say?" "No," and
before I could say anything else I was treated to
a sound which I would get to know very well;
something like a cross between a chuckle and a
snigger. "We'll arrive on April 14th. I'll stay
on but the other two will check out Friday
morning."

As he talked, I was trying to determine if we
could provide accommodations for all the dates
he required. As it turned out, Brian didn't mind
switching rooms several times, despite having
copious quantities of clothing as well as
several pieces of scientific equipment too
complex for me to describe to you. Finally, it

was determined that we could, indeed, provide accommodations for Brian's stay. "I'll send your confirmation today Mr. Carling," I said. "Great!" was the response; "Don't worry about the mud." And he hung up.

As good as his word, Brian and "friends" arrived on the appointed day. Edie Gair, girl geologist, (young, dark- haired and a real knock-out) arrived in a rental car; Scott McQuown (tall and ruggedly handsome) was driving a boxy 4 wheel-drive vehicle and Brian (chunky of build with a great smile) roared up in an extremely muddy company truck. (Was this a portent of things to come?) The trio was pretty tired that evening so there was little time for socializing. They were to be an early-rising group (coffee on the table by 6:30 am, breakfast at 7:15), all of whom enjoyed a hearty breakfast.

Everyone was up bright and early the next morning except the sun. It was raining! As we served breakfast, Brian and Edie explained that the wetter the job site, the muddier it would become. (And it certainly did!) At this point, Bob went to the back porch to get a boot tray which, he announced to all, would be on the front porch for muddy boot deposits. Scott mentioned that he was expecting several packages of equipment which could be left on the porch when they arrived.

(This turned out to be 13 LARGE packages and
containers which filled most of the porch. One
piece weighed over 200 pounds and only made it to
the porch because a caring motorist leaped from
his car to help us and the Fed Ex lady move that
sucker.) Edie announced that she expected a bad
hair day and off they went to the muck and mire of
the abandoned landfill.

The week passed quickly, if soggily. We were
favored with rain every day that week. Happily,
parts of each evening were spent getting to know
"the kids" as we called them. Edie, we learned,
is a geologist and one of Brian's bosses. After
her departure he confided, "Edie is very good at
her job and I enjoy working with her a lot."

Scott worked for a company that had been sub-
contracted to, as best I can describe it,
X-ray the job site. Brian's task was to
supervise the drilling crew and install water
wells to provide samples from specific
locations. Scott's X-rays would insure that no
gas or oil lines were punctured by the drilling
crew, since a mistake would literally be the end
of Brian. We also learned that the F.B.I. had
once asked if Scott's company would be available
to X-ray a suspected Mafia burial ground in up-
state New York. We never learned if they took the
job, as Scott is, rightfully, square jawed and

closed mouthed about his company's activities.

Brian left us the first weekend. He was off (I forget where) to watch his idol, Bill Elliott, race his Thunderbird in a NASCAR event. ("Number 94, Bob, just in case you watch the race," instructed Brian.) Mr. Elliott lost, and upon his return, Brian sadly explained, in detail, why. Actually it was a lucky break for us having Brian out of town. It meant we could relocate his things (except his trail bicycle which was on the patio) to a temporary location, make up his room for pre-booked weekend guests and have his freshly made up room in the "Roost" ready for his occupancy when he returned. **Note:** The sun shone brightly the two days while he was gone. Was a trend developing?

Brian stayed with us for 39 days and nights the first go round and it rained 33 of those days. Carol commented one morning that the weather was "taking on Biblical proportions and perhaps we should think about renting an arc". It became so difficult to work in the landfill that Brian purchased a set of fishing waders. This made sloshing about in the mud an easier task and meant less clean up before coming home to "Mom and Dad" as he called us.

Brian is quite tidy and I'm pleased to report that he brought no discernible droppings into the Inn.
We did have to hose down the porch daily, but this was a small price to pay for the pleasure of his company.

Chadds Ford is located about twenty minutes from Philadelphia, so Brian was ill prepared for the vagaries of small town living. Early on in his stay he came back from dinner with a puzzled look on his face. "Am I dressed funny or something; do I look OK to you guys?" he asked. Carol and I assured him that he looked fine. "Are you sure? At the restaurant people kept staring at me." Carol laughed. "People stared at us a lot when we first came to town. They're just trying to figure out who you are and what you're doing here. Eventually they'll get to know you and stop looking you over."

 It happened even sooner that we predicted. Brian went out to dinner at a spot featuring a karaoke night and had a great time and (no doubt) a few beers. He came home the next day smiling and not a little bemused. "It's amazing! At lunch the waitress winked and said, 'Understand you really tore it up last night at the karaoke'; lots of people were smiling and nodding; a couple of girls, total strangers, said, 'Hi Brian'". He paused, "Suddenly, I feel like a native." Over the course of his stay, Brian got to know our town and became friendly with sundry people. In fact, a few of them would gather on the sidewalk in front of the Inn when Brain sat on our front porch playing his guitar and singing. (Was it his talent or their curiosity?)

As good as the food may be, there are just so many times you can eat at the same restaurant in a compressed period of time. In search of "palate diversity" as he called it, Brian drove sixteen miles south to the village of Beverly in search of new foods to devour. When he returned he said the food was fair and his fingers were sore. He explained that he had finished dinner and was dawdling over desert

when he spied a sizeable group of men and women, each
carrying a musical instrument, moving into a back room
and setting up for what turned out to be a jam session.
Brian is not shy. He went back to ask if he could listen
and was invited to sit down. The music ranged from
country, to bluegrass, to blues. After a while, one of the
men came over and asked if Brian played any instruments.
An extra guitar was available, and in his hands for the next
several hours. This explained the sore fingers. "I had a
great time," he bubbled and went off to bed.

Brian's first visit was for 39 nights, another lasted 23
nights, add several one & two-nighters and you have a
grand total of 72 nights. We truly enjoy having him about
the house. When he leaves us, we feel like parents sending
our child off to school. At one point on his first visit,
Carol joked, "If this lasts much longer, tell your Mom and
Dad we're going to formally adopt you."

**Brian enjoyed our breakfasts, so we were a little
surprised one evening when, in a mournful tone of
voice, he said, "Guys, I've got to cut back. I'm
putting on weight! From now on, Monday through
Friday, it's a bowl of naturola with sliced
banana, no toast, one muffin, and a large orange
juice (he never drinks coffee or tea) and that's
it. Saturday the works, with the three cheese
puff and Sunday the apple pancake, OK?"
Naturally, whatever Brian wanted was OK with us.
Brian's favorite, my 3 Cheese Puff With Baked Ham
recipe, follows.**

CAROL'S 3 CHEESE PUFF WITH HAM

6 eggs
1 cup ea.:   grated Monterey Jack & Sharp Cheddar Cheese
1 cup cottage cheese
1/4 cup flour
1/2 teaspoon baking powder
1/4 teaspoon salt
4 Tablespoons melted butter
1/2 cup finely chopped baked ham

Preheat oven to 350°. Beat eggs until light & fluffy. Add remaining ingredients & stir gently until well blended. Pour into two greased 8 inch round baking pans. Bake for 30 minutes or until browned. Cool slightly in pans, remove and use pizza cutter to cut into four wedges from each pan. Garnish with fresh parsley sprig and serve. (serves 8)

TWO ON THE AISLE

October is a beautiful time of year in this part of Ohio. The sun shines brightly and the woods and hills are ablaze with color. It was October 3rd, 1995; the town clock had just tolled twelve; the sun was shining and I was puttering about in my little herb garden. The phone rang and I dashed into the kitchen to answer. I prefer that anyone calling the Inn speak with me or Bob rather than an impersonal, and sometimes infernal, machine.

Trying not to sound winded, I picked up the

receiver. "The Outback Inn Bed and Breakfast, this is Carol." "Do you have cats?" said the caller. "No", I stammered. "We're a Bed and Breakfast." "Oh, I know that," came the response. "What about dogs, birds, any type of pet?" "None; we offer a smoke and pet-free environment," I answered, trying for a little humor. From the other end, an appreciative chuckle. "That's a good line. Great, my allergies won't kick in; so, if you have a room available, my wife and I would like to book it for the 15th." We had, so they did, and that was my introduction to Edwin H. (call me "Sy") Sypolt.

Sy and Betty (short for Elizabeth) arrived early evening on Sunday the 15th. In just minutes they had signed our guest book, settled into the Hooray For Hollywood Room and were downstairs anxious to get acquainted. They were our only guests that night and terrific company. Some of the people who stay at the Inn seem more like family than guests. It was that way from the beginning with Betty and Sy.

In short order we learned that Sy had worked for the Upjohn Company and Betty had been a nurse specializing in working with stroke victims or patients with cerebral injuries. They were helping their daughter Leslie, son-in-law Dan and three grandchildren Nicole, Kyle and Lee

settle into their new home. They were also
international travelers and enjoyed attending
theater.

"There are no mediocre productions in any of our
area theaters. In Cincinnati we have nothing but
hits! Good, bad or indifferent, at the end of the
play, the musical, the opera, or a kindergarten
Christmas program, these uninformed boobs all
around us leap to their feet and applaud like it
was the greatest thing since chopped liver,"
fumed Sy. Betty nodded her head vigorously.
"I've never seen anything like it. We were at the
opening production of The Globe Theater in
London and saw a very, very good production of *A
WINTERS TALE*. You know, as good as that
production was, the audience just applauded
enthusiastically, but they remained seated. And
so did we," she added.

The four of us were in total agreement that a
standing ovation was something that had to be
earned. It was an audiences' reward to the
performers and technical people, musicians,
etc., for an outstanding, amazing presentation
and for coming as close to perfection as is
humanly possible. If indulged in habitually and
haphazardly, the standing ovation loses all
meaning.

Several months later Sy called and said, "Leslie's cat lives
and if you want us to keep coming to the Inn I suggest that

you both pray that the furry devil lives long and prospers."
If ever two couples were a natural fit, it was the Sypolts
and the Belfances. Sy and Betty were interested to know
about Carol's and my theatre and broadcasting careers and
we were interested to know about them and about the
many trips they have taken around the world.

Sy and Betty have stayed with us a half dozen or more
times. They send us information on the productions at the
Cincinnati Playhouse In The Park. Once Sy called to say,
"God, where were you guys when we needed you! We saw
a superb production of *SWEENY TODD* and had no one
to share the experience with. It's one of the best
productions we've seen in years, anywhere. For whatever
reason, some of those boobs in the theater were actually
walking out during the first act. ("Boob" is a word that Sy
is fond of, but uses only when the shoe fits.) As usual, the
show got a standing ovation and, for the first time, Betty
and I stood and applauded, too, because AT LAST we had
just seen a show which actually deserved a standing O."
Because Sy and Betty usually stay mid-week or Sunday
nights during most of their visits, we have had the good
fortune to have the Sypolts mostly to ourselves. Prior to
one visit Betty called to ask if we could eliminate "this one
time" eggs, ham and bacon from their breakfast. She
explained that she was now part of a study group
comprised of post-menopausal women and needed a
breakfast that was essentially made up of juices, fresh
fruits, and grains. "'Carol can just give us a larger fresh fruit
cup and some toast," was Betty's suggestion. "No big deal,"

I said; "Carol has a slew of great recipes. She'll surprise you with something yummy." And, of course, she did. Along with the usual choice of juices, Carol served a fresh fruit cup with a cheddar-parsley mini muffin on the side, toasted English muffin bread and Carol's Apple Crisp.

CAROL'S BREAKFAST APPLE CRISP WITH A TWIST

6 medium-size apples, peeled, cored and thickly sliced*
1 cup regular oats
2 cups naturola cereal (available at most health food stores)
1/4 cup honey
1/4 cup brown sugar
1/4 cup flour
1/2 teaspoon each: ground cinnamon and nutmeg
1/2 cup butter, melted

Heat oven to 375°. Grease an 8x8x2 inch pan. Combine apples (*preferably Granny Smith and Golden Delicious), honey, brown sugar, spices, 1/2 cup of the oats and 1/2 cup of the naturola. Spread mixture in pan. It will need to be packed in firmly. Mix remaining oats and naturola with flour and pour on melted butter. Toss with fork to combine. Spread crumb mixture evenly over top of apples. Bake until fruit is soft and top is golden brown and crunchy - about 45 minutes. Portion into servings bowls and serve with warm skim milk to pour over top. (Serves 6)

THE GAME'S AFOOT

Early in November of 1994 I received a call from a charming woman, Doris Barg of Akron, whom I had

never met when we lived in that city. Doris,
however, was familiar with Bob and me from our
work in the theater. She had recently read an
article about the Inn by Frances B. Murphey, a
popular columnist and travel writer for the
Akron Beacon Journal. " My husband and I want to
give the Inn a try. Jack and I relish finding
B&B's where the Innkeepers are fun to stay with.
Those are places we enjoy revisiting regularly,"
she said. Because of some work going on upstairs,
I booked them for a two night stay in the
downstairs Roadside Roost and, happily, we have
had the pleasure of their company at least once a
year ever since.

You need to know that, at this time, we were
totally redecorating the upstairs Hooray For
Hollywood room. The wallpaper used by the
previous owners was a hideous pattern of large
powder blue and white roses on a bilious blue
background with large silver swirls; this in a
room that had featured twin brass beds. The clash
of the wallpaper and the brass beds was so loud
that you could hear it downstairs.

This is a long-winded way of saying that the new
Art Deco wallpaper was up and painted.

I know, you're asking yourself, "Why paint wall
paper?" Well this "paper", which we had ordered
from England, is actually a vinyl material

with a raised pattern and must be painted after installation. No sweat, I thought, and Bob will be so surprised and grateful I've finished the room that he'll take me out to dinner. Who could know that this form of vinyl is extremely absorbent and that small white (seemingly unpainted) dots would appear daily for about a week, requiring vigilant touch ups.

Monday, November 14th, 1994, will be forever etched in my memory. I had planned my day perfectly. The fruit for Tuesday morning was cut and in the fridge, mini-muffins were baked and I was "dressed for action". That is to say, I was wearing Bob's zip-front coveralls which were paint spattered, several sizes too large, but cool to work in. To keep paint blobs out of my hair, I had already donned an old New York Yankee baseball cap of Bob's that he used when painting. Looking back in my mind's eye, I doubt that I looked like your typical Home Ec. major at work in the kitchen of her B&B.

All was in readiness upstairs. With drop cloth down, masking tape in place, ladder in position, all that needed to be done was to stir the paint and begin, so I did. Bob describes me as a "careful painter". What he really means is that I don't slop paint everywhere, don't have to clean up splatters of paint and, thus, I'm slower at painting but <u>much quicker</u> at clean up!

The painting went well that day. There was no reason to rush. Doris had said, "We should arrive sometime after four and before five." I estimated that I would be finished and ready for a shower by two or two-thirty at the latest. And, "glory be", at two-twenty-five I had hung up my cap and was about to go upstairs for my shower when, what to my wondering ear should I hear, but voices out on the porch and to the front door drawing near.

"Ding-Dong!" No, it was not Avon calling; it was Doris and Jack Barg.... and I was "trapped".   I couldn't hide; they could see me through the beveled-glass front door, frozen in their line of sight.   Dressing in overly large, paint-spattered coveralls is not my way of creating a good first impression but I had no choice. Opening the door and trying to smile, I murmured, "You're just a wee bit early." As I ushered them in, Jack dead panned, "Nice outfit, did you get that locally?" Doris laughed heartily and said, "Jack behave! Carol, with luck, you'll get used to what he thinks of as humor."

I knew then and there that we would hit it off beautifully. People with whom you can share laughter are people to be truly treasured. Bob was still commuting weekends from our home in Akron so he did not get to meet Doris and Jack on their first visit.   The three of us spent those

two days getting to know one another. In the
"ain't it a small world" category, I learned that
the Bargs had been members of the Firestone Park
United Methodist Church and knew my mom and dad,
Olive and Roy Parker, as well as numerous other
"Park people" whom I had known for much of my
life.

On Tuesday we decided to kill two birds with one
stone by timing a visit to the Stockport Mill
late afternoon and then going on to have dinner
together. We enjoyed our visit to the historic
old Mill and were interested to learn that, at
one time, electricity for the Mill and the
village was provided by water power. A portion
of the Muskingum River was diverted through a
narrow trough under the Mill, creating a strong
current that rotated the generator and created
electric power.

I had read about a restaurant south of
McConnelsville that used to be a riverfront
warehouse. It was said to have a scenic view of
the river.

Several members of the Morgan County Historical
Society had mentioned that the owner was "a mite
eccentric" but always "put on a good spread".
We were the only people in the restaurant that
evening and our dining experience can best be
described as unforgettable.

What we encountered upon entering the restaurant
was largely what had been described to me by
Morgan County friends and neighbors. There was
railroad memorabilia, several types of kerosene
lamps, an interesting array of photos from "the
old days". A collection of pitchers was on a
shelf and there were several old signs that
advertised products long gone from the market
place. And there was dust.... lots of dust.

If this restaurant had been located in a larger
community, most likely it would not have been
allowed to operate. There was a potentially
beautiful view of the Muskingum but it was
difficult to see the river because the murky
windows needed a good washing. I looked over at
Doris and smiled wanly; she shrugged, gave me a
"what the heck, we're here" look. So we sat down
to what we would later refer to as our "fish and
chips from hell" dinner.

I'm not sure that dinner is the correct
nomenclature for our meal. It consisted of fried
pieces of fish (origin and species still to be
determined) and potatoes, also fried. No
vegetable was served and no salad offered. Doris
enquired about rolls or bread. Rolls were
delivered by our serving person from her apron
pocket and one per person was unceremoniously
plopped on each plate. Jack laughed out loud.
When the check arrived we learned that the rolls

were "extra". Jack laughed again. We went back to the Inn and partook of healthy doses of bicarbonate of soda. Bob called that night to see how things were going and I told him of our "evening out". Bob laughed out loud! I was not amused!

I finally got to meet Doris and Jack when they spent their first of several Fourth of July holidays with us. They usually stay four days. On the Fourth of July weekend the local Jaycees and Chamber of Commerce sponsor a rubber duck race on the river, an auction, bingo, a carnival and food fair "on the square", live entertainment and top off the holiday with an excellent fireworks display. Sitting on our front porch steps affords you a perfect view of the display. Carol usually serves homemade lemonade.

Doris and Jack are never bored. They are "gamesters". They share a passion for cribbage, Mah Jong, and crossword puzzles. They are experienced travelers, both domestic and ship travel (at least two cruises every year).

Each has respect for the other's personal interests, too. If you ask, they will tell you that Jack's fascination with jazz groups and Big Band musicians or Doris' fondness for cross stitch projects and collecting recipes are "just part of what we do".

Making the culinary rounds on cruise ships twice a year tends to sharpen one's taste buds. We are pleased that the "Barg Good Housekeeping Seal of Approval" has been awarded to Carol's Orange-Vanilla French Toast.

CAROLS ORANGE VANILLA FRENCH TOAST

12 slices French bread, 3/4" thick
2 teaspoons pure vanilla extract
6 eggs
1 teaspoon orange zest
3/4 cup orange juice
1/4 teaspoon salt
1/2 cup milk
3 Tablespoons Triple Sec
2 Tablespoons Sugar

Grease two, 9 inch by 12 inch glass baking dishes and place cut bread slices in a single layer. In a large bowl, beat eggs, orange juice, milk, sugar, vanilla, orange zest Triple Sec and salt until well blended. Pour over bread, turning slices to coat completely. Cover and refrigerate overnight.
Bake in preheated 450° oven for fifteen minutes, carefully turning after ten minutes has elapsed. Sprinkle with confectioners sugar.
(serves 4)

FE, FI, FO, FUM

I had just come back from shopping when the phone rang. I answered in the usual way and a gently-accented female voice came over the line. "Good Morning. I am calling from Texas and I would like to enquire about securing a room for my husband and me. We are planning to visit my daughter, son-in-law and grandson for a week in June." I explained that the Roadside Roost room had a double bed, the Hooray For Hollywood room featured twin beds and the Queen's Chamber contained a queen-size, four poster bed. "Well, we probably should have the Queen's Chamber because we are large people," she said.

Mental images of childhood visits to circus sideshows, where I stared in awe at "giants" and "the fat lady", flashed through my mind. I tend to wince mentally when a never-before-seen guest suggests that they or their spouse is a "large person". This is because we once had a guest who said over the phone, " We better take the Queen's Chamber because I'm a pretty big guy". When the gentleman arrived, he so thoroughly filled the doorway, the room darkened visibly. Big was not how I would describe this man. Enormous would be more apt. Bob surreptitiously substituted a more substantial chair at the dining room table and made sure that this guest was its' occupant when breakfast was served.

At first, Bob had thought of butting two chairs together for him to use. "Mr Big" and his not-very-large wife stayed three nights. Each evening when we went to bed, Bob and I included our furniture in our evening prayers.

As it turned out, our "giant" caller, Ketta Weinstein, is about five feet two inches tall and husband Miguel just slightly taller. You can imagine my reaction when I greeted our very

"large" guests from Texas. "Oh," I said, "Oh". I
was totally nonplussed... "Do come in," I
fumbled.

Describing this couple as petite might be an
overstatement but, by no stretch of anyone's
imagination, could these gracious individuals
be described as large or even bulky. Ketta was
much too polite to acknowledge what, I am sure,
were raised eye brows and a mouth agape. "Thank
you", she said and Miguel smiled amiably as they
entered the Inn.

The Weinstein's are a thoroughly engaging couple
from The Woodlands, located not far from
Houston.   Ketta's speech retains more than a
hint of Mexico where she grew up and attended
college. Prior to her retirement, Ketta taught
high school students commercial business
courses.

Miguel's accent is totally different from
Ketta's, but just as intriguing. Born in
Hungary, and a young boy when Hitler came to
power in Germany, Miguel and his family were
forced to flee from Europe to save their lives.
Fortunately they were able to join relatives who
had settled in Mexico City and, once there, begin
a new life. Miguel's family ran a successful
delicatessen and, eventually, several
businesses related to the automotive field.

The next morning after breakfast Ketta rose from
the table and began to clear the dishes away.
"No, No, Ketta," I said, "You and Miguel are our
guests; I'll clear the table". "Well, all right
if you say so, but yesterday you said that your
home was our home away from home. In my home I
clear the dishes from off the table." Several
days later Ketta took a sip of her coffee, winked
at me and purred,"You know Karul, I very much
like this clearing away of the dishes; it is very
easy to get used to." Ketta called me Karul
(pronounced CAR - and UL rhyming with hull). It
was one of several charming mispronunciations in
her vocabulary that frustrated her but I enjoyed
hearing. She would shrug and say, "I just cannot
get your name to come out of my mouth the way it is
supposed to sound. I can hear that it is not
correct but, no matter how hard I try, it comes
out wrong."

Linda arrived early one morning and we
introduced her to the Weinsteins. "Thank you for
keeping our room so clean and tidy," said Miguel.
"Yes, this is something else it is easy to get
used to," added Ketta. The next day as Linda
arrived Ketta asked, "Lean-dah, do you eat?"
Linda looked a little puzzled but replied, "Oh
yes, last night Rhett and I had fried chicken,
mashed potatoes, corn on the cob, and a salad and
then later we went out and picked up a big pizza."
"You are so trim Lean-dah! I would love to look

that thin again. I hate being so big." Linda
gave me a "is she kidding me" look and I
explained, "Ketta is convinced that she is a
large person. She must think that I'm the size of
a Texas longhorn." "No, No Karul, you are tall,"
she paused; "I think we should talk of other
things, OK?" Linda and I solemnly nodded in the
affirmative and the subject never reared its
ugly head again.

Miguel and Ketta proudly introduced their daughter
Claudia, son-in-law Jeff and grandson Joshua to us. The
five of them spent the week touring the area's historical
landmarks, visiting Amish country and enjoying being
together and basking in the fine weather. "The air is much
lighter here, Bob," remarked Miguel. Around Houston at
this time of year there is much humidity. It is nice to walk
in the sunshine and not perspire immediately."

Joshua seemed to have taken special enjoyment from his
visit to *The Wilds,* North America's largest conservation
facility (14 square miles of reclaimed strip mining land).
This innovative institution's mission is to support wildlife
conservation through education programs, scientific studies
and the development of management techniques. Animals
at *The Wilds* live in protected, large open-range habitats.
There are no bars, cages or pens in sight and mini-busses
take visitors on a one-hour guided tours. Bactrian camels
(two humps), Asian wild horses, gazelles, white
rhinoceroses, giraffes and zebras are pointed out as tour

guides also explain *The Wilds'* efforts to preserve these and other species from around the world. Each year more of our guests tour *The Wilds* while they are in the area.

It is always a challenge to provide a variety of breakfasts for guests who are staying for a week or more. Carol thought that since Ketta and Miguel lived in Texas it might be fun to do a "Tex-Mex" style breakfast for them. Since Miguel was not allowed to have whole eggs in his diet, Carol adapted her Eggs Ranchero Omelet. It was a big hit with them and continues to be one of several favorite "Karul" concoctions.

CAROL'S EGGS RANCHERO OMELET

2 Tablespoons olive oil
4 eggs or 8 oz. of egg substitute
3 Tablespoons ea.: chopped red and green sweet peppers
1 teaspoon dried cilantro
1 Tablespoon water
2 Tablespoons chopped celery
1/4 Cup grated Monterey Jack cheese
1/2 teaspoon salt
1/4 teaspoon ground cumin
2/3 Cup mild salsa

Warm salsa in small pan over low heat. Meanwhile, heat 1
tablespoon oil in large nonstick skillet over medium heat. Add red
and green chopped peppers, chopped celery, 1/4 teaspoon <u>each</u> salt
and cumin. Saute 5 minutes or until vegetables are tender.
Transfer to small bowl, cover and keep warm.

Whisk together eggs (or egg substitute), cilantro, 1 Tablespoon
water, 1/4 teaspoon salt and 1/4 teaspoon cumin. Heat 1
Tablespoon oil in same skillet. Add egg mixture. As omelet cooks,
using spatula, gently move cooked mixture to center and allow
uncooked mixture to flow into bottom of pan. When cooked,
omelet should be barely brown on bottom and soft and moist in
center.

Spoon vegetable filling over half of omelet. Sprinkle grated
Monterey Jack cheese over vegetable mixture. Flip other half over
top of filling. Gently divide in half and slide onto two warmed
plates. Serve with warm salsa on the side. (serves 2)

HAVE GUN, WILL TRAVEL

Friday - July 14, 1995

The sun rose bright and hot. In just a matter of hours Union and Confederate troops would be entering Morgan County and preparing to do battle. The temperature Thursday had been in the mid-90's in the shade, if you could find any. The weather forecasters were predicting even higher temperatures for the weekend. The big battle would occur on Sunday. The two armies dressed in full wool battle uniforms would wage war in a natural amphitheater and it would be hot... throat-parchingly hot.

At the Inn we were on a full alert. We were prepared for the worst. Our air conditioning was A-OK operational and our rooms were cool, comfortable and ready for the occupation. Carol had made lemonade, ice cubes were in ample supply, hoses were attached to the main water supply in the event that officer's horses needed to be cooled down. All was in readiness: nothing was left but to await the incursion of the troops for Morgan County's Civil War Encampment Days.

Expected for the weekend were John and Connie Barnes, Tim and Chris Park and Jeff Keith who was bringing several horses with him. We never met Jeff or his horses. The weather was simply too hot for them to be part of the weekend activities. Mark Barnes, John and Connies' son, stayed with us instead of Jeff. Mark usually slept in his enlisted man's pup tent encamped with fellow re-enactors but this weekend he would be grateful to "come home" each evening to his air conditioned room and a shower. This was Carol's and my introduction to Civil War Re-enactors. These hardy souls turn back the clock to those troubled times, to live and drill as army personnel. They sleep in tents, cook their meals over camp fires and often re-enact the life of a specific person they have chosen to portray. In some cases it is a husband and wife from history, or a single man, perhaps a girl with a boyfriend in the army or an entire family with little children. What amazed us was how authentic everything was. Military uniforms, women's dresses with pantaloons, hoop skirts and bonnets, various types of rifles, pistols, swords, mess kits, canteens, buttons, boots were either antiques from the Civil War period or faithful reproductions.

The McConnelsville Re-enactment Weekend is very popular with many re-enactment groups. Members of the Morgan County Re-enactors Association work long and hard to ensure that bathing and rest room facilities are readily available, camping sights are clearly marked, and special parking areas for vehicles and live stock are provided. Townspeople and merchants also lend their support to the event which attracts many Civil War history buffs to the village.

NOON - Friday - Temperature in the 90's
Across the river at the Malta Park, recruitment speeches are being made by representatives of the Union and the Confederacy; a number of men enlist. Approximately thirty minutes later Carol calls from the living room,

"Bob, come here, there's a big gun parked in front of the Inn." Sure enough, a beautifully polished Gatling Gun loaded onto a trailer is in full view, as are John and Connie Barnes who are mounting our porch steps.

TWILIGHT - Friday - Cooler
The army recruiters are gone from Malta Park. An ice cream social is in full swing but the sounds of officers barking orders can be heard in the park and from across the river in McConnelsville. Six artillery batteries are setting up on both sides of the river. When ready, probably under cover of darkness, they will begin firing on each other's positions.

Now the moon is out and the cannons have commenced firing. The first salvo comes in five second intervals from Confederate cannons one, three and five. The Union cannons respond with a barrage of all six cannons fired at once. Almost instantly Confederate cannons two, four and six return fire in unison. Up and down the valley the thump, thump, thump of the artillery reverberates against the hills; the echoes slowly receding into the darkness. The powder rats, young boys in uniform, scurry to each cannon with a new powder charge and the bombardment goes on for about an hour, and then all is quiet.

SATURDAY - JULY 15, 1995 - Hot! 99 degrees!
John and Connie are dressed for the parade and out of the
Inn right after breakfast.

He has learned that he will be a Union Sergeant this
weekend. John travels with Union and Confederate
uniforms and "joins" the army in need of armament to
"even-up" the battle when it begins.

Carol and I stroll up to Main Street, find some shade and
watch the parade. Then we move up to the Court House
and watch the presenting of the colors and the 21 gun
salute. The men, in their wool uniforms, are drenched with
sweat. On the steps of the Court House are gathered
President Abraham Lincoln and Generals Ulysses S. Grant
and Robert E. Lee. The generals make short speeches
about the "brave and honorable men serving in their
commands. President Lincoln offers a speech he made at
the dedication of a cemetery in Pennsylvania.

Carol and I agree that the gentleman playing Lincoln
catches the essence of the persona and offers a masterful
performance of the Gettysburg Address. Additionally, the
entire scene is enhanced by the back drop of the historic
buildings on the Town Square. The architecture ranges
from 1828 through 1890 and lends an authenticity of time
and place.

**By afternoon the heat was so intense the general
order goes out to the re-enactors that the men
can wear their red shirts without jackets.**

The ladies in long dresses keep their hoop skirts but remove their pantaloons for comfort. Bob and I stroll down to the encampment under umbrellas to provide our own shade.

Many of the tents were pitched in The Grove under massive maple trees that provided welcome shade. Across the street on The Commons, the sutlers had pitched their tents. A sutler, we learned, was a civilian provisioner to an army post, often with a shop on the post. During the Civil War, sutlers also were found at army camps near the front lines. They sold goods to the soldiers that were unavailable through the army quartermaster, such as tobacco. It was a dangerous life and many sutlers were killed by cannon fire or when the opposing army attacked the camp.

The sutlers at McConnelsville offered every conceivable item that a civilian might need such as hoop skirts, pantaloons, bonnets, toys and sasparilla. It was also possible to purchase a full uniform, officer or non-com, as well as side arms, rifles, mess kits, canteens and other items needed by soldiers.

Twilight - Cooler, but still plenty hot!
After dinner we found our lawn chairs and walked over to the Baker House located two blocks from the Inn. People were assembling there to listen to the Morgan County Civil War Singers perform a cantata comprised of songs sung by both sides during the war. The selections were well chosen and ably performed.

Following the concert a formal military ball was held under the stars, for all in uniform to enjoy.

Sunday - July 16, 1995 - Temperatures in the high 90's
Breakfast for our troops at 8:30 today, allowing plenty of time for them to get to church services. Carol, Linda and I rush to do the laundry, wash the dishes, clean and make up the guest rooms and our public rooms. We are anxious to experience the battle re-enactment at the Richmond Farm. We arrive at the battle site in plenty of time, pull up a couple of hay bales, sit down and await the battle.

There is no way to truly describe the re-enactment. Initially, it's like watching battle scenes from *Gone With The Wind* without the close-ups. Your first impulse is to pick out the people you know. You want to see them in action. John is the easiest to find because of the Gatling gun. A little later we see Mark and other soldiers moving against the enemy. There is a heated exchange of gunfire, Mark staggers and falls to the ground. He does not get up, and there is no medic to offer treatment.

Suddenly the sounds and sights of the battle seem more real, the guns louder. What you witness is not the spectacle, but the horror of war. You begin to comprehend the depth of bravery it took for a man to charge across an open field toward enemy lines, volley after volley felling friends and comrades as he races forward with no thought of retreat.

And then it is all over. A solitary bugle plays taps, the
"dead " rise, brush off the dirt, cannons are loaded onto
trailers, uniforms packed, and these weekend soldiers are
ready to go home. Shouts of "See you next year" or "Let
me know about that sword" can be heard as they leave and
very soon Doc Richmond's farm is a homestead again.

John and Connie have stayed with us for every re-
enactment weekend since 1995. Mark went back to
his tent, but usually stops in to say hello. John
& Connies' other son Mike is not a Reenactor, but
we hope to meet him . Connie is very down-to-
earth in her approach to life. She has a mirthful
little smile that creeps across her face when she
is amused. John is an easy going, folksy kind of
guy who always seems to have something bubbling
in the back of his mind. He's an inventor but not
an eccentric.

The summer of '96, when John and Connie arrived,
he handed me a business card.   "Johnathan W.
Barnes is the name, and guns are my game," he
drawled. Connie smiled, "Show Carol your sample
case," she said. I read the card, which smacked
of the 1860's, and learned that "Johnathan"
represented the manufacturers of Gatling guns,
Henry Repeating Rifles and Remington Pistols.
"That little two shot is just the one for you."
John leered comically and pointed to a small
silver pistol holstered in a very fancy ladies
garter.

I gave him a haughty look, flipped a shoulder and replied, "Just what I need if I ever open a dance hall or gambling joint Johnny Boy." Connie broke into peals of laughter and John chuckled at my response.

The next day he and his "assistant" Connie put on a sharp shooting act at The Grove that was great fun. He had found a way to create the illusion of real bullets hitting a target while firing blank rounds. "How did you do that?" I asked. "Trade secret he replied."

Later that day, as we sat on the front porch reminiscing about our days as kids growing up, Bob mentioned that one of his childhood disappointments was that he never was able to have a Whizzer Motor Bike. "There was one boy in our village who had a Whizzer. He was a little older than me and under no circumstances was he going to let me ride his bike. I never did get to ride one and I never got to own one either." John said, " Well if you're over our way you can stop in and hop on. I've still got a couple left. I had over a dozen restored and running at one time". Bob smiled, "I didn't realize that people were collecting Whizzers." "Connie and I started writing a little news letter for 13 of us in Ohio, and pretty soon we were the National Vintage Motor Bike Club with over thirteen hundred members.

"Connie was Secretary and she wrote and published a quarterly news letter. When the club began taking up too much time, we backed off some and let others handle those chores."

John is just like my late Grandpa Vineyard. When Grandma wanted cabinets for the kitchen he'd respond by saying, "Well let me study on it." It wasn't very long before he'd "figgered it out." Once the materials arrived, he'd start whistling and working and singing a bit too, and soon Grandma had exactly what she'd asked for. John recently built two cannons to go along with his Gatling gun. He also builds early flintlock muskets identical to those used in the 1600's by the Pilgrims.

The summer of '97 John and Connie were Doctor and Mrs. Johnathan Barnes, MD. Bob and I went down to The Grove and watched "Doc Barnes" work as an Army doctor. John had "studied on it" and had designed and constructed false arms and legs as well as fingers for the "wounded" to wear. He could then perform surgical procedures used during the Civil War with realistic accuracy. The screams of pain and the sound of a surgical saw ripping through a leg bone (actually a three inch plastic plumbing pipe) was frighteningly realistic. While John treated his patients and

The Queen's Chamber

Roadside Roost

Hooray For Hollywood

The Opera House, 1892

Town Square & Court House, 1920's

Howard House Restaurant

Morgan County Herald, publishing since 1844

Gloria Meranda waiting for her tiles to cure.

John Wells, State Rep. Nancy Hollister & Bob, Celebrate Winning A $400,000 Grant For Downtown Revitalization

Brenda de la Mora Teaching For Children's Arts Program

"Firearms Salesman" John Barnes & His Gatling Gun

Bob Honored For Community Service

Larry Grodsky And His "Sturdy Steed"

Professor Jack Working "The Peanut Gallery"

Lynnette & Carol As They Appeared In "CHICAGO"

Bob & Carol Perform their Cabaret Show **"FROM ADAM & EVE, TO MASTERS & JOHNSON IN 2 ACTS"**

explained to them what he had to do, we observers
shared in a realistic moment of "living history"
that dramatized what wounded men faced if they
made it from the battlefield to the medical
tent.

Carol and I always look forward to seeing Connie and John
because we never know who they'll be or what new
activities they're into.

I like cooking for John and Connie. They both
enjoy home style cooking and appreciate
breakfasts made from "scratch". So, I always try
to create a new recipe each time they visit.

CAROL'S SCRAMBLED EGGS IN TOAST CUPS

Bread Cups

8 slices whole wheat bread, crusts removed
2 Tablespoons butter or margarine, softened

Scrambled Eggs

2 Tablespoons butter or margarine
2 Tablespoons chopped fresh chives
2 Tablespoons chopped fresh parsley
7 eggs, whisked
Celery salt, to taste
Regular salt & fresh-ground pepper, to taste
Grated Cheddar cheese

To prepare bread cups, cut off crusts and flatten bread slices with rolling pin. Spread butter on one side of each slice. Picking up the corners, gently press bread, buttered side down into 8 muffin cups. Bake at 350° for 12 minutes, or until lightly toasted.

Meanwhile, melt butter in large skillet. Add beaten eggs, chives, parsley, celery salt, salt and pepper and cook over medium-low heat until softly scrambled.

When bread cups are done, increase oven temperature to 475°. Fill cups with scrambled eggs, top each with grated Cheddar cheese and return to oven about 2 minutes, or until cheese melts. (Serves 4.)

THE "POOTER" QUEEN

Have you ever met an energetic, highly charged person with a fabulous sense of humor that's just slightly "off center"? Angie Righi fits this description to a tee and her friend and co-worker, Susan Reineki, is just as much fun. These spirited young ladies have stayed with us twice when business brought them to McConnelsville. They are a truly memorable pair of gals and, in Angie's case, a magnificent mischief maker.

Angie is a petite blonde from Blue Springs, Missouri; dark-haired Susan is the taller of the two and hails from Independence. They were in the county to install computer software for a local company. Training various personnel at the company was also part of their assignment. Brian Carling, whom you've already met, was with us at that time ... which meant we had three "jokesters" in residence for the week.

As a fun sideline, Angie formerly toured shopping malls and county fairs selling *THE POOTER*. A pooter is a cylindrical device made of a pliable plastic material. It is flesh colored, about two inches in height and approximately one and one half inches in diameter, with a hole at one end. The pooter will fit comfortably against the soft portion of your hand directly below the thumb while hidden in the palm of your hand. When positioned properly and squeezed to force air out of the cylinder, a sound that can politely be described as a "social indiscretion" is emitted. It reminded Bob of the old "whoopee cushion" that was a popular practical joke years ago. A pooter, however, if properly manipulated, will produce an amazing range of pooter blasts. Keep in mind that we were totally in the dark regarding pooter lore at this time. It was only after the girls had visited one of our local watering holes that we became "pooter cognizant".

Susan and Angie are big fans of the Kansas City Chiefs football team and football in general. It was a Monday night and Susan said, "Bob, Angie and I are going up to that sports bar we saw, and catch the game on a really big screen." They left and I recall saying to Carol, "Two attractive young women, unescorted, at our local sports bar? I'm betting they won't be sitting alone for very long." Carol chuckled, "Bob, Angie is married, Susan is engaged; they'll deal with whatever develops."

A little later Brian drifted in. "Hi, been across the river playing pool, the smoke finally got to me so I came home." He grinned. "Where are the girls"? Carol jumped in with, "Brian, you've just touched on a sore spot with Papa Bob. Angie and Susan went to The Chatter Box to watch the game and he's worried about them." Brian looked puzzled. "Why"? I was about to respond when the girls staggered through the front door laughing hysterically.
"If only someone could have video taped it! The expressions on their faces were too much. The bartender

was totally losing it," bubbled Susan, who again succumbed to merry salvoes of almost uncontrollable laughter. The two of them sat down on the edge of the couch. Angie wiped the tears from her eyes and filled us in on what had taken place. "We were just sitting at the bar having a beer and watching the game. There weren't any seats at tables and you could see the game better sitting at the bar, anyway." Susan piped in, "So, there we were, and, totally unsubtly, these two guys in tee shirts and tattoos sat down on either side of us." Angie's expression spoke volumes. "These guys, on the looks scale, were a three. We tried to get them to understand that we were not interested and totally unavailable." Susan spoke up, "I think the tall one with the long hair thought he was McConnelsville's answer to Fabio."   Angie started giggling. "We tried to be polite but nothing we said or did seemed to be getting through to them. They were sticking to us like a couple of used car salesmen."

Susan said, "Finally we were forced to resort to the pooter strategy." I looked at Carol; Carol looked at Brian, and Brian looked at me. Brian finally asked, "What the heck is the pooter strategy?" Susan continued: "Well, Angie put her arm across her tummy and leaned into the bar." Angie demonstrated the movement and said in her sweetest voice, "Oh, I think I need to go to the little girl's room." It was at this point that she "pooted".

The sound was loud, plosive, drawn out and unmistakable ! We sat in stunned silence. Angie said in a sweet, little-girl voice, "Oh, I think I'd better go <u>right</u> <u>now</u>!" She rose and took several steps away from the couch in demonstration. Susan told us that as soon as Angie was out of ear shot, the long-haired lothario leaned toward his buddy three bar stools away. "She's NAS-TEE," he hissed! They chugged what was left of their beers, slid quickly from their stools and hot-footed it out the front door. Angie and Susan paused, expecting us to share in their merriment.

The three of us tried to smile but, frankly, were somewhat aghast. None of us had ever met anyone who could do THAT on cue before! Seeing our discomfort, Angie and Susan burst into fresh peals of laughter. Finally, Angie held up her left hand and gave us our first glimpse of her "personal pooter". She then did about a ten minute demonstration of the full range of her pooting prowess, from long and raucous to short and stacatto! The sounds she produced were diverse and increasingly hilarious. Laughter built on laughter until we were literally "laughed out". Carol remarked, "If laughter is therapeutic, we should be healthy for the next six months!"

The topper for their bar room misadventure occurred when Angie returned from the restroom. She revealed the existence of her pooter to the patrons of the bar. The more she pooted for them, the more they laughed. "They howled so loud I had to cover my ears," Susan said. Brian remarked, "This tale will be told and retold for years to come. Those two 'studs' will never live this down; they'll be razzed about this forever."

So far it looks like Brian was right. Every so often a total stranger sees me and asks, "What do you hear from those pooter girls?"

We purchased several pooters from Angie to use as gag gifts. Brian has one and we've heard he's become quite a pooter, too.

Susan and Angie were very fond of my Pear Puffed Pancake and perhaps you will be too.

CAROL'S PEAR PUFFED PANCAKES

3 eggs
one large pear
1/2 cup milk
1/2 teaspoon ground nutmeg
1/2 cup flour
1 Tablespoon sugar
1/4 teaspoon salt
1 Tablespoon lemon juice
4 Tablespoons butter, divided
Nutmeg Sugar

In a bowl beat eggs until blended. Add milk, flour, nutmeg, sugar, salt. Whisk until combined. Cover and refrigerate overnight. Peel, core and slice pear thinly. Toss with lemon juice and cover. In 11" ovenproof skillet, over med.-high heat, melt 2 T. butter, remove from heat and pour in batter. Arrange pear slices over batter in a spiral pattern, from outer edges to center. Bake in pre-heated 375° oven for 15 minutes. Melt other 2 T. butter. When pancake is done, drizzle butter on top and sprinkle generously with the nutmeg sugar. Return pancake to oven and broil for 1 minute. Put on warmed serving platter and cut into pie-shaped wedges. Serve immediately. (serves 2)

PART THREE

"BREAKFAST AT THE OUTBACK"
or
Talk! Talk! Talk!

CAROL CASTS OUR BREAD UPON THE WATER

It all began quite innocently. In the fall of 1995 the Morgan County Chamber of Commerce sponsored a Business Fair. "Bob, I volunteered you as Master of Ceremonies for the first ever Business Fair," said my lovely lass. This was said, not surprisingly, after an excellent dinner she had prepared. "A post to which I have always aspired", I replied, kissing her lightly on the cheek.   "Oh, and I forgot to mention, Carol, I received a call from a gal on their door prize committee this afternoon. I said we'd be pleased to supply three loaves of your poppy seed citrus bread as door prizes. Was that OK to do?" This earned me a mildly sardonic smile along with, "Actually, as newer members of the Chamber I think its a good idea that we participate; it sends out a positive message. Plus I know I can count on you to zest the oranges and lemons and create attractive labels for the packaging."

We set up a small table at the Business Fair and dutifully manned our "booth" . Our door prizes were prominently displayed, we chatted with visitors, passed out our promotional brochures and magnetic business cards and got to know some of our local business men a little bit better. The exhibit to the left of our booth was loaded with telephones and other communications equipment and was manned by Jim Kelly of Sprint. He took one look at Carol's bread and quickly registered for our door prize drawing. More about Jim later.

One of the visitors to our booth was Mike Cullums, the News Director for radio station WMOA located in

Marietta and the sister station of WJAW our station in McConnelsville. Mike is a genuinely nice guy with a smooth baritone vocal register that's ideal for radio news casting.   We chatted about the Inn, and I encouraged him to register for our door prize drawing. He filled out a coupon and left to visit other booths.

As fate would have it, Mike Cullums and Jim Kelly each won a loaf of Carol's bread. Jim was present and received his bread at the drawing. Mike had a deadline to meet for his news report and was long gone. Carol reminded me we were planning a trip to Marietta in several days; "why don't we drop the bread off at the station on our way down town?" I suggested. I called WMOA, "Bob Belfance from The Outback Inn B&B. Surprise and congratulations Mike, you won our door prize. Carol and I will be in Marietta on Wednesday; when's a good time to drop off your bread?" We decided to meet right after his last morning news cast.

I had taken the bread from the freezer and we were ready to leave when an idea struck me. "Bob, why don't I take our demo tapes with us. We might be able to do some free lance commercials for the station." Bob's upper lip stiffened perceptibly, then a slight sneer crossed his face, "You're good baby, you're real good!" He hates to admit it, but Bob's Bogie impression, on a scale of one to ten is about a three. Suffice it to say, we took our demo tapes with us that morning.

When we arrived, Mike took us on a quick tour of
the station and we talked "radio" for awhile.
Bob had not mentioned that we had been doing
commercials in the Akron/Cleveland market.
While listening to our tape, he began to laugh at
the humor in one of our spots. "I always wondered
who voiced that series of spots. I was very
impressed when I heard them. John Wharff our
General manager is out just now but I'll make
sure he hears them." We left soon after and spent
several hours in Marietta. Leaving nothing to
chance, when we returned to the Inn, Bob wrote to
John Wharrf III at the station. This letter
sparked a phone call and a meeting at the Inn.

JOHNNY THREE

Mr. John Wharff, III
General Manager
WMOA/WJAW

October 30, 1995

Dear Mr. Wharff:

I had hoped to meet you when Carol (my wife) and I stopped by the
station. We dropped off a door prize that Mike Cullims had won.
(he can explain) I always catch your show in the a.m. and wanted to
see the "face-behind-the-voice".

By way of introduction, let me say that I have been in and around
broadcasting since I was nine years old. My wife and I are both

AFTRA members and you have probably heard our voices on the air around Ohio. We purchased the Outback Inn Bed And Breakfast a little over a year ago and now live in McConnelsville.

Mike mentioned that you are attempting to establish a stronger sales and broadcast presence in McConnelsville. I don't know how we might establish a mutually beneficial relationship but if you're interested... Lets talk.

I am currently directing the play *LOVE LETTERS* at Muskingum College. My daytime schedule is flexible so if you'd like to chat call me at **1-800-542-7171**.

Yours truly,
Bob Belfance

The meeting took place the following week. John Wharff, III appeared to be in his early thirties with an easy smile and an enthusiasm for radio that is rare in the younger generation today. We consumed copious quantities of coffee during our brainstorming session and spent a pleasant afternoon together.

Mr. John Wharff, III

November 10, 1995

Dear John:

Thanks for stopping at the inn to chat. Carol and i enjoyed meeting you.

THIS IS CAROL BELFANCE AT THE OUTBACK INN BED AND BREAKFAST SAYING, THANKS FOR LISTENING TO WJAW, YOUR QUIET ISLAND IN McCONNELSVILLE AND ALL OF SOUTHEAST OHIO.... needless to say we'd be pleased to do it.

November 14, 1995

Bob & Carol Belfance
The Outback Inn Bed And Breakfast

Dear Bob & Carol:

A note of thanks and thoughts from our meeting of Last Wednesday.

"Breakfast At the Outback on WJAW" featuring Bob and Carol Belfance of McConnelsville's The Outback Inn Bed And Breakfast ... a weekday hour long program featuring news of interest in McConnelsville with a different local guest each day. Tune in every Monday thru Friday from 9:06 a.m. - 10:00 a.m.

Questions to be answered:

1. Is there enough material, guest prospects to fill 5 hours a week for an indefinite period of time?

2. Are there six sponsors that will pay for prime local advertising?

3. Quality production from facility??

Some thoughts for measure, did enjoy the coffee and conversation.

Sincerely,
John

November 20, 1995

Dear John:

I have always believed that the old saw "crawl before you walk, walk before you run" made sense.
The idea of doing the breakfast show has merit but Carol and I both feel that a one hour format, five times per week, is too ambitious a project to open with. A more conservative approach would allow all of us to develop the show and eventually build to the format you suggest.
     1. Why not consider Monday & Friday Programs, 30 minutes in length. There would be no problem material/guest wise.
     2. Given the format change, I think I can find sponsors.
     3. If you are able to supply a recorder and two mikes I am confident that we can achieve good broadcast quality from the dining room table at the inn.

We will be in Akron from Wednesday the 22nd. thru Saturday the 25th. visiting friends and relatives and eating copious quantities of turkey,so you can contact us any time from Monday the 27th, on.

Regards from us both,
Bob

As is usually the case, refining the format, securing the equipment, contacting potential sponsors and "making the sale" took longer than anticipated. In addition we had guests at the Inn prior to Christmas and all Christmas Week. Bob was able to get things moving again after the holidays. He created a simple sales piece. Correspondence with Johnny Three, (our nickname for young Mr. Wharff) continued at a pace until one day, thanks to Rod Gallagher (President, First National Bank of McConnelsville) and Sprint's Jim Kelly (remember him?), we had sponsors.

January 22, 1996

Attention Johnny Three:

Enclosed is a copy of the sales piece I used to sell ***BREAKFAST AT THE OUTBACK.***

Our sponsors for the first 13 week segment are:

Sprint
Attention: Mr. Jim Kelly
Community Development Director

First National Bank of Mcconnelsville
Attention: Ms. Naomi I. Wright
Vice President & Director of Marketing

I indicated that we were shooting for a March 4th air date but made no hard promise regarding our time frame.

Regards,
Bob

February 6, 1996

Hi! Ho! Johnny Three:

Since our projected air date is March 4th I thought it prudent to get in touch.

QUESTIONS: 1. HOW ARE WE DOING ON EQUIPMENT?
                        2. WHEN DO WE "TRAIN" ON THE EQUIPMENT?
                        3. WHAT ABOUT PROMOS FOR THE SHOW?
                        4. I HAVE A MUSIC CUT FOR THEME WHEN DO WE CUT SHOW'S OPEN/CLOSE?

We should talk soon.

Regards,
Bob

Getting our show on the air took a little longer than we anticipated. There were delays in securing the equipment, which delayed the training process as well as the rehearsals or "dry runs" prior to taping our first show for broadcast. A calming influence throughout this process was Bob Crock, Vice President of WJAW as well as Station Manager. He was always ready, able, and willing to do whatever was needed to coax the process along.

At long last we were ready to go. At 8:30 a.m., April 29,

1996, *Breakfast At the Outback* took to the airways. I
said to Carol after our first broadcast, "I wonder if anyone
will listen?" Carol's upper lip stiffened, a slight sneer
crossed her face and she said, "Of course they'll listen.
We're good baby; we're real good." Carol knows exactly
how to break me up. "OK, OK, I admit it, your Bogie is
better than mine."

**Dear reader, after 416 glorious broadcasts,
BREAKFAST AT THE OUTBACK is, temporarily, off
the air. WJAW is now an affiliate of ESPN Radio.**

**When Bob and I agreed to do the show we set goals
we hoped to meet. We wanted to give listeners
factual information about happenings in the
county. Making people more aware of the fine and
performing arts, promoting the village's needed
Downtown Revitalization project, and promoting
Economic Development and Tourism were high on
our list as was building 4 new schools for our
young people (now under construction).. We were
successful beyond our wildest dreams!**

We're grateful to Jim Kelly of Sprint and Rod Gallagher
and Naomi Wright of the First National Bank. They
stepped up and sponsored our show in the belief that it was
worthwhile and would have popular appeal. And they were
right...... So, now its time to pop our CD into your boom-
box and meet a gathering of our friends and guests.

PROFESSOR JACK

My first recollection of Jack Bennett is that we were introduced at a "fish bowl cocktail reception" in the miniscule lobby of the Weathervane Community Playhouse. I say fish bowl, because you are on view for the members who have come to see "that New York Director we hired". You smile, try to appear comfortable, and are forced to listen to "live resumes", one-by-one, from almost all assembled. Attendance at these events will vary depending on when auditions are scheduled. If the casting date is more than two weeks away from the reception, you can count on being invited to dinner almost every night until auditions begin. Once you have posted the cast list, be sure your larder is well stocked or you will surely starve to death. Jack was polite and charming and made no attempt to impress me with his theater bio; in so doing, he made a lasting impression.

Jack was in the company of a petite, energetic little lady of indeterminate age, with jet black hair and an infectious laugh. She was Billie Lahrmer, long-time director of The Coach House Theater at the Akron Women's City Club. Jack was one of Billie's "stable" of actors who performed only in Coach House productions. It would be almost 20 years before Jack would appear in one of my productions.

Jack was well known to local television viewers as Professor Jack, host of a delightful television show that brought youngsters into the studios of WAKR for after-school fun and frolic.

Evenings, during the six and eleven o'clock news, Professor Jack's weather report combined the necessary facts with his droll sense of humor. It was in this context that we first worked together.

The Sunday afternoon following Thanksgiving, 1962, Jack called me at home. "Mr. Belfance, this is Jack Bennett calling. I don't know if you remember me, but we met when you first arrived in Akron. It was a reception at the theater." "I remember very well. You introduced me to Billie Lahrmer and were the only person who didn't try to overwhelm me with your performing exploits." Jack laughed, " I don't know if that's good or bad Mr. Belfance." "Definitely good, it said a great deal about your character. And please, call me Bob; Mr. Belfance is my father. What can I do for you?" "I'm desperately looking for a new Santa Claus to appear on my show. Mine just died." After a *longish pause* I said, "If you like, we can meet at the theater and go through my casting files. Will you need someone on a daily basis?" "I'll need someone Monday through Friday, with the last day being the 24th." "Jack, your show airs when most of my actors are at work and that could be a problem." *Another pause.* "I was hoping that you would consider playing the role," he said. "I'll supply the Santa suit, of course, and I think the pay is pretty good, too." *A longer pause.* "When would you want your Santa to begin?" "At approximately 4:15 tomorrow," was the quick reply. *A really, really long pause.* "Jack, I'm one of those people who is very superstitious so, tell me truthfully, who wore the Santa suit last." My question totally broke Jack up. He laughed for about 30 seconds.

Finally he gained control and said, "Bob, for you, it'll be a new suit." I played Santa daily for about four weeks and had a great time adlibbing with Jack.

Jack and I were undergraduates at the University of Akron when the only things being smoked on campus were the free sample cigarette packs passed out by the manufacturer's reps. I was a wee little freshman and he was a "Big Man On Campus" junior. The very first time I appeared in a show with Jack I performed a tap routine in a variety show sponsored by the Student Council. Jack was Master of Ceremonies for the show and did some very funny stand up humor throughout the show. The next time I saw Jack he was lip synching records for a teen music show on WAKR TV.

What has come to be known as Bob's, "Ernest & Delia / Daisy" cycle began in the spring of 1981. Bob cast Jack and me in a production of *HOLD ME!*, a non-musical revue comprising sketches based on selected stories and cartoons by Jules Feiffer. In one of the sketches Jack was Ernie and I was his wife Daisy.

Next Jack and I spent a great deal of time together in bed eating pilchards as Earnest and Delia in *BEDROOM FARCE*, a delightful British comedy by Alan Ayckbourn. Pilchards are sardine-like fish and were to be served to us on toast.

Jack and I loathed the idea of eating these foul smelling, ugly little things. Fortunately theatre is essentially illusion and Bob's Prop Crew created what looked like pilchards but was actually a very edible concoction of non-fishy food stuffs. The production was a huge success. One of the critics described Jack as "walking about like a befuddled penguin".

Several years later we were Daisy and Earnest in *THE MAN WHO CAME TO DINNER* a 30's drawing room comedy by two of America's great playwrights, George S. Kaufman and Moss Hart. Bob said that I was almost the second coming of Billie Burke and Jack reminded him of Gayle Gordon who was always loosing his cool on *OUR MISS BROOKS* and *THE LUCY SHOW.*

Bob directed a short film about the effects of divorce on a typical family called *REMEMBER THE CHILDREN.* In this film, Jack and I appeared as the children's grandparents and by this time area audiences were convinced that Jack and I were old marrieds. The film, produced by the Summit County Domestic Court System and the Child Guidance Center is required viewing for all couples filing for divorce. Ironically, Valerie Griggs, who gave a moving performance as the young mother in the film, received a notice to attend a screening as part of her divorce-in-progress. When she arrived, the psychologist

took one look at her, said, "you're"...., and
pointed at the blank screen of the monitor.
Valerie nodded and smiled weakly. "Your
performance in the film is very moving. I don't
think you need to watch it; you've lived it," she
said and sent Valerie on her way.

The first production Jack played in for me was the musical
revue *SIDE BY SIDE BY SONDHEIM*. Jack has a knack
of playing comedy in a wonderfully understated way. Our
audiences were captivated with his dry and devilishly
sophisticated delivery. Over the next five years Jack earned
several acting awards for his performances in *THE
DINING ROOM, COLE, PAINTING CHURCHES, OUR
TOWN* and an original musical revue which I wrote called
DIVAS, DAMES AND DOLLS.

Early on, Jack stayed with us at the Inn. One morning at
breakfast he remarked, "Bob, this reminds me of when we
did *BREAKFAST WITH LES AND BESS*!" "Oh my God!
You're right!" said Carol. *BREAKFAST WITH LES AND
BESS* is a lightweight comedy by Lee Kalcheim. The play
deals with the misadventures of Les and Bess, a married
couple who co-host a radio talk show from their New York
City penthouse. "I guess we've been so busy with guests at
the Inn and guests for our show that I never picked up on
the similarity," I responded. Carol was laughing as she
remembered Jack's cameo performance, "Jack, the audience
loved you in the play. You were the most adorably funny
drunk I've ever seen on any stage."

Long-time friends are a very special treasure.
Jack remembers me when I was young.... and thin.
Amazingly, Jack looks pretty much the same as the
guy I met at the Student Union in 19 ... something
or other. When I play the tape of Jack's
appearance on our show, for me, it conjures up
many, many delightful memories.

COVER GIRL

Paula Carr Reece visited us with her cousin
Frances Helmick in the fall of 1996. She was born
in Malta, as she says," By mistake, really. My
mother came up from Parkersburg to visit her
sister and suddenly I decided it was time to make
my appearance." An elegant lady with a smooth-
as-silk voice, Paula also proved to be loaded
with surprises.

Paula graduated from Marietta College and was
very active in their theater department. She
also was one of the founders of the community
theatre in Parkersburg and also performed at the
local little theater in Marietta. It turned out
that Paula worked for our sister station in
Marietta, WMOA, and was the hostess of a weekly
fifteen minute radio show. "It was what, in
those days, we called a *Woman's Show* and was
sponsored by Bonhams Department Store. I
covered no controversial topics and featured
helpful homemaking hints, fashion trends,

makeup tips and, of course, the latest news about hair styles. In other words, I was a shill for Bonhams women's clothing, makeup and housewares departments and their in-house beauty salon."

Eventually, Paula worked her way up to the position of Casting Director at CBS Television in New York.

"In those days five of us handled the casting for just about all their shows. I remember casting a very young Charlton Heston in tiny roles on soap operas and weekly dramatic shows. It was obvious that he would go on to bigger and better things.

"My fondest memories are of Edward R. Murrow. I hardly knew him, but he was such a presence. Whether you saw him in the halls at CBS or on camera he was impeccably dressed, always smoking a cigarette of course, and he always had a smile and warm hello for his co-workers. Ed Murrow won my admiration when he laid his career on the line and took on Senator Joseph McCarthy. I wonder how many people today are aware of what a devastating effect McCarthy had on the entertainment industry in the 1950's. An actor or actress simply accused (in most cases falsely) of being a Communist, was blacklisted from appearing in films or on television. Although you were not, and had never been, a communist, if your name wound up on the list

secretly circulated to the casting departments
of motion picture studios and television
networks, your career was dead in the water. It
was a terrible time in the history of this
country. One shudders to think what would have
happened if Ed Murrow had lacked the courage of
his conviction."

Carol and I looked forward to "chatting up" Paula during
her stay with us. One morning after leafing through the
scrap books we maintain about the Inn and our activities
she opined, "You both have quite an extensive background
in theatre and radio." "Yes, Bob even owned a theatre
once," said Carol. Paula smiled, " Don't tell Frances, but
theatre is my favorite art form. (Cousin Frances is an
accomplished artist.) "Where was your theatre located?"
"You've probably have never heard of it. It was a small
non-star summer theatre near the beach, just three miles
due south of Plymouth Rock." Paula clapped her hands
together, "The Priscilla Beach Summer Theatre, on White
Horse Beach in Manomet! Correct?"

Our jaws dropped and two mouths stood agape. I
recovered and asked, "How is it that you're familiar with
the theatre? It's certainly not high on the list of Straw Hat
Theatres... in fact, when I bought it in 1969, it was damn
lucky to even make the list." "You may find this hard to
believe, but in May of 1939 I appeared on the stage of that
theatre playing the title role in *VICTORIA REGINA*."
"Talk about the proverbial small world," I said. "I wonder
what the odds are of you acting at Priscilla Beach, and

being a guest at the B&B of a former owner?"
Paula smiled, "There's something else you may find interesting about my time at the theatre. One night early in the run I was backstage in a space that served as my dressing room, touching up my makeup. This tall, thin man wandered in smoking a pipe and carrying a large pad."

"OK if I sketch you as you make up?" he asked. "Sure," I said. "He didn't say much after that but I could tell he was sketching furiously.

"The Stage Manager called places and I explained that I had to leave to begin the show. I was curious to see what he had drawn. May I see what I look like?" I asked.   He smiled shyly and said, 'Maybe later, when it's in better shape.'" Carol poured us more coffee and asked, "Did you ever get to see what he had drawn?" Paula nodded, "Yes I did. In full color on the cover of the August 5, 1939, edition of *THE SATURDAY EVENING POST*." Two mouths were again agape. Carol stammered, "But... but... that means that you sat for Norman Rockwell!" "That's right.... as you said, it's a small world."

We sat speechless as Paula finished her coffee and then went out on our front porch. Southeastern Ohio was ablaze with color that fall and Paula enjoyed watching the sun play across the trees on the hills across the river. It was several weeks later that we began kicking ourselves for not remembering that sitting on our coffee table, buried under several other books, was ***NORMAN ROCKWELL and THE SATURDAY EVENING POST - THE***

MIDDLE YEARS, 1928-1943. We rushed to the living room, opened to the index, and on page 159 we found Paula, as beautiful then as she is now. The illustration was entitled ***SUMMER STOCK.***

YOU ARE THERE

On December 7, 1941, I was running my *20th Century Limited* electric train at breakneck speed around its figure eight tracks. My parents were off somewhere and I was staying the afternoon with my God-Parents, who were also my Mom's sister and brother-in-law, Sadie and Vernon Ruska. They shared a two family house with "Grandma and Grandpa In-The-City", my mother's mom and dad. My father's folks were called "Grandma and Grandpa On-The-Farm". I can still smell my Aunt Sadie's chili cooking and hear the chatter of my train careening around the tracks. There was music playing on the radio. My Aunt Sadie was in the kitchen and Uncle Vernon was reading the Sunday newspaper.

Suddenly, the music stopped and a man started talking about air planes dropping bombs. This caught my undivided attention because, at that time, I wanted to be a stunt pilot just like the one my Dad and I had taken a ride with in August, on my birthday. I remember my Aunt rushing into the living room; her face was very white, and she was crying and wringing a red and white striped dish towel in her hands. My Uncle sat transfixed; the newspaper was in his lap and he was staring at the radio. And, I remember looking from one to the other, but they seemed to have forgotten I was there. Aunt Sadie sat next to my Uncle Vernon and he put his arm around her and said very quietly, "It'll be all right honey," and she cried even harder.

It was not all right! By the end of World War II millions of innocent people had been exterminated. Hundreds of thousands of America's sons and daughters, fighting to preserve our freedom, were killed or maimed. My memory of the little white banners with gold fringe that hung in the windows is still vivid. A blue star on the banner meant that someone from that family was in one of the armed forces of our country. If the star was gold, you knew that someone from that family had been killed in action. I remember the first gold star in Grandma-In-The-City's neighborhood. I was riding my tricycle on the sidewalk when I saw Mr. Bonifede, a kindly old man who lived across the street. He was standing in front of a house about a block away. As I rode up to him, he removed his hat, crossed himself, knelt on the sidewalk and began to pray. I looked where he was looking. In the window hung a banner with a gold star. It's strange the things you do when you are young. Grandma-On-The-Farm had a banner with four blue stars in her kitchen window for my Uncles: Eddie, Frank, Freddie and Roy. When we went to see my grandparents I always sneaked out by myself to check the color of the stars on that banner. When the war ended all four stars, thank God, were still blue.

This is a roundabout way of introducing you to Hank
Kenderdine and his wife Bonnie. They have stayed with us
numerous times and always come bearing gifts. Sons,
Hank Jr., a judge and David, a school teacher, have also
graced our hallowed halls.

Hank is an inveterate hunter and once brought us
some venison. Bonnie always packs a generous
five pound bag of giant pretzels baked in
Lancaster, Pennsylvania, not far from their home
in Elizabethtown. We have also been favored with
an array of jams and jellies. Really delish!

We wanted to include a portion of Hank's
appearance on our show because his vivid
descriptions of the bombing of Pearl Harbor are
almost poetic. As he recalled his involvement in
the events of that day we had a feeling that we
had shared the experience with him. Hank will
not admit to it, but some of his actions on
December 7, 1941, were truly heroic.

TWO BROADWAY BABIES

Many of our guests ask,"What are you two doing in
McConnelsville?" I suppose it is because our
background suggests a big city or major market
life style. The same question could be applied
to two of our most favorite people and special

friends, Mary Felver and Dolores Parker Morgan.
Mary, an outstanding Broadway actress, married
her late husband Ralph, a prominent Attorney,
and moved to Akron, Ohio. Bob has often
mentioned to me that he had the greatest respect
for Ralph, whom I never had the opportunity to
meet.

 Dolores, a wonderful vocal stylist, sang and
toured with (among others) Duke Ellington prior
to her marriage to a most elegant gentleman whom
we both adored, the late Doctor E. Gates Morgan.
Dolores met Mary when she, too, settled in Akron.
Eventually, they became fast friends.

I have had the pleasure of directing these ladies and they
both are consummate professionals. I last directed Mary in
a production of **DRIVING MISS DAISY**. Her
performance in the title role was breathtaking to behold.
Mary so totally submerged her persona, that her closest
friends were hard pressed to find "Mary" on stage. While I
did not direct **THE BELLE OF AMHERST** (Mary
directed her own performance), I relished her portrayal of
Emily Dickinson in this fascinating one-woman play.   She
explored the life of one of America's greatest female poets
with unabashed passion, giving a performance that was as
finely tuned as a symphony orchestra.

Bob and I always look forward to visiting with
Mary. Attending one of her intimate dinners for

six is akin to reliving those times when civility
and courtesy were very much a part of life in
America.   If you think hard and long about it,
you may recall that vestiges of civility
survived into the 1960's. Mary brings to the art
of entertaining the same style and grace to be
found in her performances on the stage.

Dolores or "Dee" is a consummate musician with a
commanding presence in front of her audience. She
possesses a vocal sound that is as sweet as honey.
Dee has a special sensitivity when it comes to interpreting
the lyrics of a song. Her phrasing is born of experience and
a deep-seated need to communicate the "story". When
these elements blend with the playful sensuality she
exudes, it makes for a "knock out" musical experience. I
had the opportunity to experience Dee's professionalism
when she starred in **DIVAS, DAMES AND DOLLS**, a
musical revue which I wrote, produced and directed. I
have to believe that if Cole Porter or Irving Berlin had
heard Dee's renditions of their songs in **'DIVAS'**, they
would have "flipped". It was no surprise that several of
Dee's numbers stopped the show nightly.

Sadly, Bob and I had only a few occasions to
socialize with Dee and Gates before he passed
away. Born in Virginia, he was the epitome of
what was once called a "Virginia Gentleman". Bob

said recently that he so enjoyed the way Gates
would greet him with, "Good evening Robert", and
he will greatly miss those melodious tones.

A WANDERING MINSTREL, AYE!

We enjoy living in Morgan County and have made
many new friends. We are pleased to count among
them, Dayle Silvus. I was standing in the check
out line at Central Market when all of a sudden
the man behind me burst into song. You will agree
that I had a legitimate excuse to step back from
the gentleman, since this type of behavior is not
usual for a grocery store check out line. As I
listened to his rendition of SHINE ON HARVEST
MOON, I had to admit that the gentleman had a
pleasing voice and that his interpretation of
the song was quite good. He finished with a very
lyric FOR ME AND MY GAL, smiled, and said "Hello,
I'm Dayle Sylvus, who are you?" I introduced
myself and we've been friends ever since.

Dayle's parents, Edwin and Mildred, owned the C. C.
Silvus & Sons grocery store in Hackney (about 15 minutes
south of our B&B). When Dayle turned six, the family
including his 4 sisters and 2 brothers, all moved to
McConnelsville.

Dayle recalls that, "At the ripe old age of nine I
went to work for Lovell's Clothing Store as an
errand boy. One of my jobs was to take men's

trousers to the home of the lady who did
alterations. I was so short at that age that they
wrapped the trousers around my arm so I wouldn't
drag them across the sidewalk. I worked there
all through my school years and moved up from
delivery boy to salesman before leaving for
service in the Army. After the service I went
back to Lovell's. In all, I worked a total of
38 years at the store. I guess I'd still be there
if it hadn't closed when folks went to shop out of
the county."

Now when Dayle and I happen to meet in downtown
McConnelsville, we exchange a big hug (Dayle is
one of the world's great huggers). We also
frequently break into song, with a few
accompanying dance steps, before continuing on
our seperate ways. So far, we haven't been
arrested as public nuisances or even looked upon
as "eccentric" by the Morgan County citizens.

Dayle is often seen in our various parades riding a
patriotically decorated bicycle like none that I've ever seen.
It looks as if he is riding on bent wheels which cause the
bicycle to bounce up and down and to wobble strangely.
People watching the parade are always delighted with
Dayle's mugging as he rides his "whoop-de-do" special. He's
retired now but stays active working for the Morgan
County Commissioners and the County Recorder at the
Court House.

119.

When we told Dayle that we'd like to do a "remembrance radio show" of what downtown McConnelsville was like when he was a lad, he more than filled our request. He got together with friends, tapped their collective memories, and arrived at the recording session armed with so much wonderful material that it took <u>two</u> shows to complete his fascinating "Memory Walk Down Main Street". We enjoyed every step and, judging from the number of enthusiastic phone calls we received, so did our listening audience.

A SPICED PAIR

Have you ever met someone and had a persistent feeling that you've known them before? It's as though they are treasured old friends whom you haven't seen in a few years. Immediately your conversation kicks into gear as you try to "catch up" on the intervening years. Granted, this is a somewhat rare occurrence, so rare that when <u>two</u> people walk through your front door and that feeling hits you, it's downright magical! On May 28, 1998, our new/old friends, Rochelle Zabarkes and David Weller stepped into the Inn, and the fun began.

We knew certain things about them before they arrived. I had talked to David when he called from New York City to book their reservations. Rochelle had recently written a book, ***ADRIANA'S SPICE CARAVAN***, which deals with cooking with spices, rubs, and blends from around the world. Rochelle's daughter, Adriana, for whom the book is named, is also its co-author. David, it turned out, was then working with Chicago City Limits, an Off Broadway acting company specializing in improvisational theater similar to Chicago's Second City. In no time, David and I arranged for him and Rochelle to appear on our radio show.

"Rochelle who admits to being slightly older than me" says David, "has had more lives than me - she's so competitive you know."

Graphic Designer, audio-visual producer, party planner, Mom of Adriana - the best job of all - one of the original spice girls (Adriana's Caravan - spice mail order catalogue), author, store owner (Adriana's Spice Caravan at Grand Central Terminal). David adds, "New lives to come include scuba diver, fossil hunter and, hopefully, grandma."

David claims, "I have had only three and one-half lives at last count. I have been an assistant chef, proof reader and a theater performer/administrator. I count that as one and one half jobs." David is from New York City. "I have set foot in 44 states. Boy are my feet tired." Speaking of feet, David also helps Rochelle when he can as she copes with all the foot traffic which comes to her shop in Grand Central.

Between the topics of cooking and theatre, with a few others thrown in for good measure, we barely

took time to sleep. I commented that if someone
would be kind enough to bring in food, we could
probably cover a few more topics! We admire
Rochelle's wonderfully upbeat attitude toward
life. Perhaps because she's a cancer survivor,
if she sets out to do something, she does it NOW
(our kind of lady)! We are so glad that David and
Rochelle have come into our lives. They have
visited here since that first meeting and we
manage to keep in touch the rest of the time via
email or telephone. We hope you, too, will find
the cuts from their radio visits with us to be
fun.

HOBGOBLINS AND MAYHEM

Shortly before Halloween in 1997 a news item
appeared in *THE MARIETTA TIMES* concerning a
guided trolley tour of several of the haunted
houses of Marietta. Guide for the tour was
Connie Cartmell, the author of a book, GHOSTS OF
MARIETTA.   I looked up from the paper, read the
story to Bob and said, "This sounds like fun."
Bob was in total agreement, a rare occurrence to
say the least, and we made plans to take the tour.

It was a dark (but not stormy) night in Marietta
when we boarded the trolley. Connie turned out
to be a thoroughly charming lady with a twinkling
sense of humor. We spent a delightful hour and a
half with her on the trolley and were treated to
"ghostly stories" about past residents and

several homes in the city. Bob and I are both
avid readers of mysteries and books concerning
unexplained phenomena so, for us, the tour was a
special treat.   Bob spoke with Connie and she
agreed to be a guest on our radio show.

Connie plied her trade as a newspaper reporter in
Chillicothe, Columbus, and Marietta for about 25 years
before writing her book. " I graduated from Ohio
University, Athens, with a B.S. in Journalism, with
specialization in business and magazine journalism.
Writing the book was something of a fluke. In October of
1992 I wrote a four-part series of ghost stories for *THE
MARIETTA TIMES* and so many people seemed to enjoy
them that I decided to do the book."

Bob and I both enjoyed reading the fifteen
fascinating stories to be found in Connie's
book. Bob's favorite concerns the story of a
killing which took place in the upstairs of what,
today, is one of our favorite restaurants; but in
those days it was a bar and notorious house of ill
repute!

GHOSTS OF MARIETTA, subtitled, Mysteries,
apparitions and hauntings of the first permanent
settlement in the Northwest Territory, is the result of years
of listening to residents tell stories about strange
happenings, jotting them down and creating some kind of
ordered sense from them. It's really what a good reporter
does when working on a story. I asked Connie if this was
an over simplification. "Not at all. I wound up with all

kinds of bits and pieces. One story might actually have come about because of stories told by three or four different people. An editor I worked for early on, always wanted multiple sources saying essentially the same thing before he would go to press with a story. Once you can get one person talking about a ghostly happening that's not too frightening, other people who have had a similar experience at the same location are more likely to share their experiences with you. Several of the stories I was told made the hair on the back of my neck stand up."

"Connie", I asked, "Do you believe the stories you have written about?" A big smile crossed her face before she answered. "It's easy to dismiss things that are difficult to explain. As I've written in **GHOSTS OF MARIETTA**....

"There are many places in Marietta that seem like they ought to be haunted. They just look that way. Conversely, there are perfectly normal, ordinary-looking houses or buildings, on seemingly ordinary streets, crawling with paranormal energy and ghostly experience. Whether or not you believe in spirits, apparitions, haunted places or supernatural energies, all of us love a good ghost story. If it's a scary story, all the better. A mystery? That works too."

THE ACTRESS

My favorite recollection of Lynette Brown is as a "rehearsal hall rug rat". I can't say for sure what her actual age was because she was always years ahead in maturity. My guess is somewhere between ten and twelve, going on forty. Her father was in my production of *THE ANDERSONVILLE TRIAL* starring a very young Ray Wise. (*TWIN PEAKS*, *ROBO COP*, etc., etc.) Lynette attended most of the rehearsals, watching and listening with an intensity that was impossible to ignore. It was also obvious that she had a big time crush on Ray, who was well aware of the situation. He treated Lynette with deference and was ever so gentle when he introduced Lynette to his girlfriend. Lynette smiled, shook hands with Ray's lady love and proceeded to tell her what a terrific actor he was. When they left, tears welled up but, trooper that she was and is... those tears never left her eyes, the chin remained firm and her cheeks remained dry. It was at that moment that I knew that Lynette was well on her way to becoming a first class actress.

Before I met Lynette, she impressed me with her performance in Bob's production of *THE BIG KNIFE*. She was playing Dixie Evans, the small but juicy role of a beautiful starlet who has fallen prey to a thoroughly immoral Hollywood producer. Her key scene was very important within the structure of the play. The audience must be touched by this frail alcoholic drug user who "knows too much" and fears for her life.

Later in the play we learn from the producer's psychopathic body guard that, "Dixie had a little accident." At that moment, the memory of this pathetic young woman, stripped first of her dignity and then her life, underscored the

tragedy inherent in the play. Lynette was able
to fulfill the intentions of the playwright in a
hauntingly fragile performance.

One Sunday afternoon, as Carol and I were driving around
enjoying the Appalachian hills of Morgan County, we got
to talking about our friends, and eventually the
conversation got around to Lynette. "You've seen Lynette
in most of my productions, what do you think was her best
performance?"

That's a tough question. She's played such a
wide range of roles. I thought she was too young
as Eleanor of Aquitaine in *THE LION IN WINTER* and
very good as Laura in *THE GLASS MENAGERIE*. If
you're talking musicals, Lynette was a knockout
in *CHICAGO* as Roxy Hart and a show stopper as one
of those wonderfully wacky women in *A...MY NAME
IS ALICE* and deliciously chic in *DIVAS, DAMES AND
DOLLS*.

And those are just a few of her outstanding performances.
I guess I've directed Lynette in close to a dozen
productions and for me her most complete and totally
professional work was as Lucia in *A SHAYNA MAIDEL*.
Audiences were totally captured by her performance as a
survivor of The Holocaust. I remember quite vividly a
performance we played for high school students.

The play began at 10:00 am, hardly a prime time for
capturing the imagination of an audience, especially one

with an average age of 17. When the house lights came up, two things were obvious: the girls in the audience were weeping buckets of tears; the boys were, too, but were trying to act macho and not let it appear that they were crying. I'm sure it was an experience those young people will remember forever. Perhaps I'm naive, but I believe that the audiences for that production left the theater with a better understanding of the human condition.

There are really two Lynette personas; the actress side of Lynette that the general public sees and hears is effusive, dramatic, and always in performance mode. The "other" Lynette reveals herself only to those special few whom she counts as her friends. <u>That</u> Lynette brings a quiet intensity to a relationship, along with a loving and caring manner which creates a solid aura of serene security ... but to those who sit in a darkened theatre, as she gently captures them in the palm of her hand and spins her special magic just for them, Lynette is The Actress.

PART FOUR

RADIO RECIPES
&
OTHER FAVORITES

LET'S COOK

It is relatively easy to host a radio broadcast from the dining room of one's B&B. Being your own producer is another thing altogether. We were always adjusting our schedule to accommodate that of our radio guests. When a guest cancelled, usually at the last minute, we were "stuck" for a show. One afternoon we wound up with no show to tape. Carol designed a recipe show based on a theme, **"Soup & Salad Suppers"** (good with homemade bread). We received many calls from enthusiastic listeners asking for more theme shows and they became a regular part of our format. Someone once said "great art often happens by accident". The same can be said for how the food portion of our format for **Breakfast At The Outback** evolved.

One show was called "Cooking Cool" and was comprised of dishes that were to be served on a hot summer day. Next was "Back To School Lunch Box Cookies". One summer there was a bumper crop of tomatoes and zucchini squash throughout our entire listening area and "The Zucchini - Tomato Show" was born. Valentines Day ushered in a show that sounded somewhat suggestive (it wasn't) entitled "Chocolate Is For Lovers". The Friday after Thanksgiving spawned our "All That Turkey" show. "Gifts From The Kitchen" ushered in the Christmas season. In Morgan County, where unemployment topped out at 19.3%, this show featured recipes that could be prepared at a relatively low cost. Bob and I, like most

129.

people, always delight in receiving gifts that reflect the personal efforts of the giver who creates something special for us.

"Fix It Fast" was popular with working mothers and single parents.

Our recipe broadcasts were influenced by our memory of the husband & wife morning radio shows of the 1940's.

In addition to the recipes, Carol offered helpful cooking tips. "Measure dry ingredients first - then wet ingredients fewer utensils means less clean up." "Put ingredients away as they are used - no question as to whether you've added them to the recipe - kitchen looks neater when you're ready to bake or cook." Carol's tips were very popular with our listeners.

Bob's irrepressible and irreverent sense of humor kept what could have been a dull 30 minutes bouncing right along. If we were doing a recipe that was a particular favorite, his groans of ecstasy in describing the entire meal were a hoot.

We enjoy cooking and are pleased to share theses recipes with you. It is our belief that freshly prepared foods are not only "dollar savers", but much more healthful and nutritious.

BLACK BEAN SOUP - WITH A TWIST

1 lb. dried black beans
1/2 lb. Kahn's Big Red Smokeys, cut lengthwise & sliced thinly
6 C. boiling water
1 T. vegetable oil
1/2 t. each: dried oregano, basil, crushed red pepper, salt
1 medium onion, chopped
3 stalks celery, sliced thinly
4 (14 1/2 oz) cans College Inn Chicken Broth
2 cloves garlic, minced
1/2 t. orange zest
1 C. orange juice
Possible topping: reg. or reduced-fat sour cream

Boil beans and water for 2 minutes, remove from heat, cover and let stand for 1 hour. Drain beans and set aside. Heat oil in large soup pot over medium heat. When hot, add smoked sausage and saute, stirring, 3 minutes. Add onions, celery and garlic and cook, stirring, 3 minutes more. Add oregano, basil, crushed red pepper and salt, cooking and stirring 1 minute more. Add drained beans and chicken broth. Bring mixture to simmer. Lower heat and cover.

Simmer soup until beans are tender, about 1 hour. Remove lid. If too much liquid has evaporated, add up to 1 cup more broth. Add orange juice and orange zest and cook 1 minute more. Makes 6 hearty servings.

CAROL'S WHITE CHICKEN CHILI

2 # boneless chicken breasts, cooked & diced (I steam them)
2 t. ground cumin
1 1/2 t. oregano
1 3# jar precooked Great Northern beans
1/4 t. cayenne pepper
1 T. olive oil
1/4 t. salt
2 med. onions, chopped
6 C. chicken broth
2 stalks celery, sliced thinly
2 C. grated Monterey Jack cheese
2 cloves garlic, minced
1 can (4 oz.) mild or med. green chilies
Salsa

Drain beans; heat oil in large soup pot over med.-high heat. Add onions & celery & saute until transparent, about 10 min. Stir in garlic chilies, cumin, oregano, cayenne & salt; saute 2 min. Add beans & chicken stock. Bring to a boil. Simmer, stirring occasionally, about 1 hr. Add chicken & cheese & reheat well. Serve with additional cheese (if desired) & salsa. Serves 8 - 10.

HEARTY TORTELLINI SOUP

4 cloves garlic, chopped
1 T. margarine, butter or olive oil
4 (13 3/4 oz.) cans College Inn beef broth
1 (8 oz.) pkg. tortellini
1 10 oz. pkg. fresh spinach, cleaned & sliced up a bit
2 (14 1/2 oz.) cans Italian style stewed tomatoes
Grated Parmesan cheese

In large saucepan, over medium-high heat, cook garlic in olive oil for 2-3 minutes. Add broth & tortellini; heat to a boil. Reduce heat; simmer 10 min. Add spinach & tomatoes; simmer 5 minutes more. Serve topped w/cheese. This is also good w/fresh sliced mushrooms added with the fresh garlic at the beginning of the recipe.
Serves 10 - 12

VELVET CORN SOUP

6 C. chicken broth
1/4 lb. med. shrimp, peeled, deveined & chopped coarse
1/2 C. diced, cooked ham
1/4 C. coarse-chopped water chestnuts
1 can (16 3/4 oz.) cream-style corn
2 t. sesame oil
1/2 t. salt
1/8 t. white pepper
3 T. cornstarch mixed with 1/3 C. water
2 egg whites, lightly beaten
1 green onion (including top), sliced thin

Bring broth to a boil in a 3-quart pot. Add shrimp, ham, water
chestnuts, corn, sesame oil, salt & pepper. Return to a simmer.
Add cornstarch mixture & cook, stirring, until soup boils &
thickens slightly. Remove from heat & slowly drizzle in egg whites,
stirring constantly. Sprinkle green onion on each serving.
Serves 6 - 8

HUNGARIAN CABBAGE SOUP

3 cloves garlic, chopped
1 14 1/2 oz. can. Italian tomatoes
1/4 lb. bacon, chopped
1 med. head cabbage, cut up
1 1/2 C. kielbasa, sliced/ halved
1/2 t. salt
5 cans College Inn Beef Broth
1 T. paprika, 1/4 C. water
1/2 C. sour cream

Cook bacon in large pot until browned. Add garlic & saute until just soft. Drain fat except for one tablespoon. Add cabbage & salt, broth & tomatoes & simmer gently for an hour. Add paprika & kielbasa & cook for five minutes. Blend flour w/cold water until smooth & stir into soup. Then stir in sour cream. Serve w/thick slices of black bread. Serves 6-8

TOMATO BREAD

2 C. tomato juice	1 t. salt
1/2 C. canned tomato sauce	3/4 t. dried oregano
2 T. olive oil	1/2 t. dried basil
6 - 6 1/2 C. all-purpose flour	1/4 t. ground rosemary
2 pkgs. active dry yeast	1/4 t. freshly ground pepper
3 T. brown sugar	2 small garlic cloves, crushed

1. Slightly grease large bowl and two 9 x 5 x 3-inch loaf pans w/olive oil. Set aside. In small saucepan, heat tomato juice, sauce and 2 T. olive oil to 120 deg. F.

2. In large mixer bowl, combine 3 cups flour w/yeast & remaining ingredients. Pour in tomato mixture & beat thoroughly for 3 minutes. Gradually add remaining 3 to 3 1/2 C. flour, mixing by hand if necessary until it holds together enough to turn out onto floured surface. The dough is quite sticky and you may need to add a tad more flour, but don't add an excessive amount or you will have a dry bread.

3. Knead about 5 minutes until dough smooths out. Place dough in greased bowl, cover & let rise until doubled in size, about 1 hour.

4. Punch dough down, let rest 15 minutes, then shape into 2 loaves & place in prepared pans. Cover pans and let dough rise an additional 45 minutes or until doubled in size.

5. Preheat oven to 375°. Bake loaves 10 minutes, reduce heat to 350° & bake 30 to 40 minutes more. Bread is done when loaves sound hollow when thumped w/knuckle. Tip loaves out immediately onto wire racks to cool. Makes 2 loaves.

COTTAGE CHEESE DILL BREAD

2 pkg. active dry yeast
1 - 2 T. dill weed (dried)
1/2 C. warm water (105-115°)
1 t. baking powder
2 t. sugar
2 t. salt
2 C. creamed cottage cheese
2 T. sugar
2 T. minced onion
2 eggs
4 1/2 C. all-purpose flour (approx.)

Sprinkle yeast on warm water; stir until blended; stir in 2 t. sugar; set aside. Combine cottage cheese, onion, dill weed, baking powder, salt, 2 T. sugar and eggs. Mix thoroughly. Add yeast mixture; mix well. Add flour to make a stiff dough. Knead on lightly floured surface until smooth and elastic. Place dough in greased bowl; turn to bring greased side up. Cover; let rise in warm place (about 85°) until double in size (1 to 1 1/2 hours). Punch down. Turn out onto lightly floured surface; knead a few times. Divide into two equal portions. Shape each portion into loaf in well-greased loaf pan 8x5x3 inches. Bake at 350° for 30 minutes. Remove from pans to rack. If desired, brush tops with melted butter or margarine. Makes two loaves.

ITALIAN SALAD DRESSING

1 C. vegetable oil
1/2 t. sugar
1/3 C. red wine vinegar
1/4 t. Italian seasoning blend
1 clove garlic, halved
1/3 t. coarsely ground pepper
1 T. grated Parmesan cheese
Pinch of crushed red pepper flakes & 1 t. salt

Put all ingredients in blender container and process until well mixed. Refrigerate in tightly covered container. Shake before serving. Makes 1 1/3 cups

THOUSAND ISLAND DRESSING

1 C. mayonnaise	1 T. chili sauce
2 pimento stuffed olives	1 t. pickle relish
1 t. minced onion	

Mix 1 C. mayonnaise with one T. chili sauce, two pimento-stuffed olives, minced, and one t. each sweet pickle relish & minced onion. Cover & refrigerate until serving. Makes 1 C.

CREAMY GARLIC DRESSING

1/4 C. mayonnaise	1/4 C. half-and-half
1 small garlic clove, halved	1/8 t. salt
1/8 t. coarse black pepper	

Mix 1/4 C. each mayonnaise and half-and-half in blender container. Add one small garlic clove, halved, 1/8 t. salt, and coarse black pepper to taste. Blend until smooth. Cover & refrigerate. Makes 1/2 cup.

BLUE CHEESE DRESSING

1/4 C. mayonnaise	1/4 C. whipping cream
1 oz. blue cheese	1/8 t. salt

Mix 1/4 C. mayonnaise with 1/4 C. whipping cream, 1/8 t. salt, and one ounce crumbled blue cheese. Cover and refrigerate until serving. Makes 1/2 C.

CREAMY CUCUMBER DRESSING

1/2 C. minced, seeded, pared cucumber
1/2 t. salt
1/4 C. sour half-and-half
3 T. mayonnaise

Mix 1/2 C. minced, seeded, pared cucumber with 1/2 t. salt. Let stand five minutes. Rinse cucumber and drain well. Mix 1/4 C. half-and-half with three T. mayonnaise. Stir in well-drained cucumber. Cover & refrigerate until serving. Makes 2/3 C.

BASIC FRENCH DRESSING

1/2 C. white vinegar
2 t. sugar
1 1/2 C. veg. oil
1/2 t. each: paprika, dry mustard
1 1/2 t. salt
1 small slice onion

Put all ingredients in blender container. Process until creamy and smooth. Refrigerate in jar with tight-fitting lid until serving. Shake before serving. Makes 2 cups

COOKING COOL SHOW
CAESAR WRAPS

4 C. Romaine Lettuce, torn to bite-size
1/3 C. Creamy Caesar salad dressing
12 oz. can of premium tuna (salmon, turkey)
1/2 C. Caesar croutons
1/4 C. grated Parmesan cheese
4 (9 or 10 in.) flour tortillas

Toss lettuce with salad dressing to coat. Add tuna, croutons and Parmesan cheese; toss to combine. Spoon salad mixture onto each tortilla near one edge. Roll up tortillas, beginning with edge nearest salad. Seal end with a small dollop of additional Caesar dressing. Cut tortillas in half to serve.

ALMOND ICED TEA

2 tea bags
3/4 C. sugar
1/4 C. lemon juice
2 C. boiling water
2 C. water
1/2 t. almond extract
1/2 t. vanilla

Place tea bags, sugar & lemon juice in container. Pour boiling water over tea mixture. Cover; let steep about 10 minutes. Remove tea bags. Add remaining ingredients to tea; stir. Pour tea mixture over ice. If desired, garnish with lemon slices. Makes 4 1-cup servings

POTATO AND APPLE SALAD

1 lb. scrubbed, unpeeled, new red potatoes cubed
1 apple unpeeled & cubed
2 diced celery stalks
1/3 C. golden raisins
1/3 C. lightly toasted and coarsely chopped walnuts

Cook 1 lb. of scrubbed, unpeeled cubed small red new potatoes in slightly boiling salted water (moderate heat) for 10 minutes or less - until just tender. Drain and cool. Combine potatoes, 1 unpeeled and cubed apple, 2 diced celery stalks, 1/3 C. lightly toasted and coarsely chopped walnuts and 1/3 C. golden raisins (submerged in boiling water for 2-3 seconds & drained well).

Mix together: 2/3 C. sour cream, 3 t. raspberry vinegar and a little salt and pepper. Pour over salad, mix well and check seasoning. Chill before serving.

SUNNY CITRUS SALAD

1 20 oz. can chunk pineapple, in juice
8 oz. med-size seashell pasta
2 oranges, peeled, chunked
1 red bell pepper, julienne-cut
1 1/2 C. julienne-cut ham
1 C. julienne cut carrots
1 C. frozen peas, thawed
1 C. cashews
Dressing:
1/2 C. orange juice
1/2 C. vegetable oil
1 T. grated orange peel
1 T. sugar
1 1/2 t. dried basil
1/4 t. black pepper
Dash nutmeg

Drain pineapple, reserving 1/2 C. juice. Cook pasta according to package directions. Combine salad ingredients in a large bowl. Combine reserved pineapple juice with dressing ingredients and pour over salad. Toss well. Cover, refrigerate at least 1 hour or overnight. Makes 6 to 8 servings.

MARINATED CHICK PEAS, TUNA & ARTICHOKE HEARTS SALAD

1 6 oz. jar marinated artichoke hearts
1 10-oz. can chick peas, drained
1 6 oz can. tuna, flaked
1 T. lemon juice
1/2 t. salt
1/4 t. cracked pepper
1/4 C. chopped red onion
1/4 C. chopped fresh parsley
1 small head romaine lettuce
2 tomatoes, cut into wedges

Drain artichoke hearts, reserving oil. Halve & place in medium
bowl with chick peas & tuna. Combine lemon juice, salt, cumin &
pepper with reserved oil; pour over chick pea mixture; stir in onion
& parsley; cover & refrigerate several hours.
Wash & dry romaine; break into pieces and place in salad bowl;
cover & refrigerate until serving time. When ready to serve, add
chick pea mixture to romaine. Toss lightly to coat with dressing.
Arrange tomato wedges around edges. Serves 4.

OLD FASHIONED LEMONADE

4 lemons
3/4 C. sugar
1 quart (4 C.) water

Cut lemons into thin slices; remove seeds. Place in a large pot and sprinkle with sugar. Let stand about 10 minutes. Then press down on fruit with a **potato masher** to extract juice. Add water, pressing fruit until well flavored. Remove fruit slices (squeezing out well with your hands before discarding). Pour lemonade into a pitcher. Serve over ice cubes. Makes 5 (1 C.) servings.

For LIMEADE: use 2 limes & 2 lemons. Prepare as above, increasing sugar to 1 cup.

For ORANGEADE: use 2 oranges & 3 lemons. Prepare as above, decreasing sugar to 1/2 cup.

BACK TO SCHOOL LUNCH BOX COOKIES BROADCAST
OLD-FASHIONED OATMEAL COOKIES

1 C. raisins
1 C. water
3/4 C. sugar
3/4 C. brown sugar
3/4 C. shortening
1 t. vanilla
2 eggs
1 1/2 C. reg. flour
1 C. whole wheat flour
1 t. baking soda
1/2 t. baking powder
1 t. salt
2 C. reg. or quick-cooking oats
1 t. ground cinnamon
1/2 t. ground cloves
1/2 C. chopped nuts

Heat raisins and water to boiling; reduce heat to medium. Simmer uncovered until raisins are plump, about 15 minutes. Drain raisins, reserving liquid. Add enough water to reserved liquid to measure 1/2 cup.

Heat oven to 400°. Mix sugars, shortening, vanilla and eggs in large bowl. Mix in raisin liquid; stir in remaining ingredients. Drop dough by rounded teaspoonfuls about 2 inches apart onto ungreased cookie sheet. Bake until light brown, 8 to 10 minutes. Immediately remove from cookie sheet. Makes about 6 1/2 dozen cookies. (These freeze well.)

GINGERSNAPS

2 C. flour
1 - 2 t. ground ginger
1 t. cinnamon
1/2 t. salt
2 t. baking soda
3/4 C solid vegetable shortening
1 C. sugar
1 egg
1/4 C. molasses
granulated sugar

Sift flour, ginger, cinnamon, salt, & soda; set aside. Cream shortening & sugar together; add egg & molasses. Add dry ingredients to the wet & mix thoroughly, then cover & chill the dough before handling further.
Heat oven to 350° & grease cookie sheets. Roll dough into 3/4-inch balls. Put granulated sugar in a small bowl & roll the balls in it. Place well apart on the prepared sheets and bake for about 12 minutes. (Cookies will puff up & then collapse.) Makes about 4 dozen.

CURRANT COOKIES

1 C. butter or margarine, softened
1 C. powdered sugar
1/2 C. sugar
1 egg
2 t. vanilla
2 1/4 C. flour
1/2 t. baking soda
1 C. currants

Combine butter, sugars, egg & vanilla; beat until light & fluffy.
Combine flour & baking soda with whisk. Stir into butter mixture;
mix well. Stir in currants. Shape into a 12-inch roll. Wrap
completely in plastic wrap; chill until firm. Slice into 1/4-inch slices
with sharp knife. Place on ungreased cookie sheets. Bake at 350°
for 10 to 12 minutes. Cool on wire racks. Makes 4 dozen.

CRISP FRUIT-FLAVORED COOKIES

3/4 C. shortening (part butter or margarine, softened)
1/2 C. sugar
1 package (3 oz.) fruit-flavored gelatin
2 eggs
1 t. vanilla extract
2 1/2 C. flour
1 t. baking powder
1 t. salt
granulated sugar

Mix thoroughly: shortening, 1/2 C. sugar, gelatin, eggs & vanilla.
Whisk together flour, baking powder & salt. Stir into shortening
mixture and combine well. Shape in 3/4 in. balls and put 3 in. apart
on ungreased cookie sheets. Flatten each with small drinking glass
that has been dipped in sugar. Bake in preheated 400° oven 6 to 8
minutes. Makes about 6 1/2 dozen cookies.

S'MORES BARS

1/2 C. butter or margarine
1/2 C. packed brown sugar
1 egg
1/4 t. salt
1/2 t. vanilla
1 C. flour
1/2 C. graham cracker crumbs
1/2 C. chopped walnuts
1 6 oz. pkg. semi-sweet chocolate morsels
2 C. miniature marshmallows

Beat butter & sugar until light & fluffy. Beat in egg, salt & vanilla.
Combine flour & graham cracker crumbs. Add to wet mixture; mix
well. Press onto bottom of greased 9 in. square pan. Sprinkle on
top, in the following order: walnuts, chocolate morsels, mini
marshmallows. Bake in a pre-heated 375° oven for 15 to 20
minutes, or until golden brown on top. Cool; cut into bars. Makes
about 2 dozen.

ZUCCHINI & TOMATO BROADCAST
HEARTY TUNA CASSEROLE

2 cans (6 oz. each) chunk-style tuna
6 oz. (3 cups) uncooked egg noodles
1/2 C. chopped celery
1/3 C. chopped green pepper
3 cloves garlic, chopped
3/4 C. mayonnaise
3/4 C. sour cream
3 tsp. Grey Poupon Country Dijon Mustard
1/2 tsp. salt
1/4 tsp. summer savory
1/4 tsp. parsley
2 small zucchini, scrubbed, sliced
1 cup shredded Monterey Jack cheese
2 - 3 small tomatoes, chopped

Drain & flake the tuna. Set aside.
Cook noodles according to package directions. Drain & rinse in hot water. Combine noodles with the tuna, celery, green pepper & garlic.
Blend sour cream, mustard, mayonnaise, salt, summer savory & parsley. Add to tuna/noodle mixture.
Spoon half the mixture into a greased 2-quart casserole. Top with half the zucchini. Repeat layers. Top with cheese.
Bake at 350° for 30 minutes or until hot & bubbly. Sprinkle each serving with the chopped tomato. 4 - 6 servings

TOMATO-CHEESE-HERB BREAD

Sour Cream Topping:
1 medium onion, minced
1 T. butter
3/4 C. sour cream
1/3 C. mayonnaise
4 oz. grated Cheddar cheese (about 1 C.)
3/4 t. salt
1/4 t. pepper
1/4 t. oregano
Pinch sage

Dough:
2/3 C. milk
2 C. biscuit mix

3 medium tomatoes, peeled & sliced 1/4 in. thick
Paprika

Preheat oven to 400°. Butter a 13 x 9 x 2 inch baking dish.

To prepare sour cream topping, saute onion in butter until tender.
Blend with remaining topping ingredients & set aside. Stir milk
into biscuit mix to make a soft dough. Turn dough onto well-
floured board & knead lightly 10 to 12 strokes. Pat dough over
bottom of buttered baking dish, pushing dough up sides of dish to
form a shallow rim. Arrange tomato slices over dough. Spoon on
sour cream topping and sprinkle with paprika. Bake 20 to 25
minutes. Let stand about 10 minutes before cutting. Makes 12
serving

FRIED ZUCCHINI

1 egg
1 T. milk
3 T. flour
1 t. salt
1 t. garlic salt
3 to 4 medium zucchini, washed and sliced into rounds about 1/4
inch thick
oil for frying

Combine egg, milk, flour, salt & garlic salt in bowl & mix well to
form batter. When ready to fry, dip each zucchini round into batter.
Fry in hot oil about 2 or 3 minutes per side, or until crisp and
golden brown. Drain on paper towels. Serve hot. Serves 4 - 6.

TOMATO ZUCCHINI PIE

1 10-inch unbaked pie shell
1/3 C. Dijon mustard
1 lb. mozzarella, thinly sliced
5 medium-size firm, ripe tomatoes, thinly sliced
2 large zucchini, thinly sliced
1/2 t. chopped garlic
1/2 t. ea.: dried oregano & basil
Salt & freshly ground pepper to taste
2 T. olive oil
Parmesan/Romano cheese

Preheat oven to 400°. Spread the mustard evenly over the pie shell, then cover the bottom completely with the mozzarella. Beginning at the outer edge of the shell, make a layered overlapping row of the tomato & zucchini slices, alternating for color. Make a second row & then use enough of the remaining slices to fill the center. Sprinkle the top evenly with the garlic, basil & oregano. Season to taste with salt & pepper & drizzle the olive oil over all. Sprinkle with the Parmesan/Romano cheese. Put the pie on a baking sheet & bake for about 40 minutes. Cool for a few minutes before cutting. Makes about 8 servings.

CHOCOLATE IS FOR LOVERS BROADCAST

OUR FAVORITE BROWNIES

1/2 pound (2 sticks) butter
4 oz. unsweetened chocolate
4 eggs
2 C. granulated sugar
1/2 C. flour
1 t. vanilla extract
2/3 C. coarsely chopped walnuts

Preheat oven to 350°. Grease & flour a 9 x 12 inch baking pan.
Melt butter and chocolate in the top of a double boiler over gently
boiling water. When melted, set aside to cool to room temperature.

Meanwhile, beat eggs & sugar until thick and lemon colored; add
vanilla. Fold chocolate mixture into eggs mixture. Mix thoroughly.
Sift flour and fold gently into batter, mixing just until blended. Fold
in walnuts. Pour into the prepared pan. Bake for 25 minutes, or
until center is just set. Do not overbake. Allow brownies to cool in
pan for 30 minutes before cutting into bars. Makes 28 brownies.

FROSTED CHOCOLATE COFFEE BARS

1 T. instant coffee granules
1 T. hot tap water
2 3/4 C. flour
1 1/2 C. packed light brown sugar
2/3 C butter or margarine, softened
2 1/2 t. baking powder
1/2 t. salt
3 eggs
1 6-oz. package semisweet chocolate morsels
Fudge Frosting (below)
Coffee Drizzle (below)
Preheat oven to 350°. Grease 15 1/2" x 10 1/2" jelly-roll pan.
In large bowl, stir instant coffee granules & water until granules
dissolve. Add flour and next 5 ingredients. With mixer at low
speed, mix ingredients until well blended. With spoon, stir in
chocolate pieces. Spread batter evenly in pan. Bake 20 - 25
minutes until toothpick inserted in center comes out clean. Remove
pan to wire rack to cool, about 1 1/2 hours. When cooled, prepare
Fudge Frosting & Coffee Drizzle. Spread frosting on coffee bars.
With spoon, drizzle Coffee Drizzle over coffee bars. Let stand
about 2 hours to allow frostings to harden. Cut into 3" x 1" bars.
Makes 50.

Fudge Frosting: In heavy 2-quart saucepan over low heat, melt 1/4
C. shortening & 4 squares unsweetened chocolate. Remove
saucepan from heat; stir in 2 C. confectioners' sugar, 1/3 C. milk,
1 t. vanilla & 1/2 t. salt until smooth.

Coffee Drizzle: In cup, mix 1 1/2 t. hot tap water & 1/2 t. instant
coffee granules; stir in 1/4 C. confectioners' sugar until smooth.

CHOCOLATE SWIRL CHEESECAKE

1 6 oz. package (1 C). semisweet chocolate morsels
1/2 C. sugar
1 1/4 C. graham cracker crumbs
2 T. sugar
1/4 C. butter, melted
2 8-oz. packages cream cheese, softened
3/4 C. sugar
1/2 C. sour cream
1 t. vanilla extract
4 eggs

Preheat oven to 325°. Over hot (not boiling) water, combine chocolate morsels and 1/2 C. sugar; heat until morsels melt & mixture is smooth. Remove from heat; set aside. In a small bowl, combine graham cracker crumbs, 2 T. sugar and the butter; mix well. Pat firmly into a 9-inch springform pan, covering bottom and about 1 inch up sides; set aside.
In large bowl, beat cream cheese until light & creamy. Gradually beat in 3/4 C. sugar. Mix in sour cream & vanilla extract. Add eggs, one at a time, beating well after each addition. Divide batter in half. Stir melted chocolate mixture into one half. Pour into crumb-lined pan; cover with the plain batter. With a knife, gently swirl chocolate batter through plain batter to marbleize. Bake 50 minutes or until only a 2 to 3 inch circle in center will shake. Cool to room temperature; refrigerate until ready to serve.

CHOCOLATE TRUFFLE LOAF
WITH RASPBERRY SAUCE

2 C. heavy cream, divided
3 egg yolks, slightly beaten
2 8-oz. packages semisweet chocolate chunks
1/2 C. light corn syrup
1/2 C. butter
1/4 C. confectioners sugar
1 t. vanilla
Raspberry Sauce (below)

Line 8 1/2 x 4 1/2 x 2 1/2 inch loaf pan with plastic wrap. Mix 1/2 C. cream with egg yolks. In 3 qt. saucepan stir chocolate, corn syrup and butter over medium heat until melted. Add egg mixture. Stirring constantly, cook 3 minutes. Cool to room temperature. Beat remaining cream, sugar and vanilla until soft peaks form. Fold into cooled chocolate mixture until no streaks remain. Pour into pan. Refrigerate overnight or chill in freezer 3 hours. Slice & serve with sauce. Serves 12.

Raspberry Sauce: In blender, puree 1 pkg. (10 oz.) frozen red raspberries, thawed; strain. Stir in 1/3 C. corn syrup.

ALL THAT TURKEY BROADCAST
SOUTH SEAS TURKEY SALAD

3 C. cooked, cubed turkey
1 1/2 C. (15 1/4 oz. can) pineapple chunks, drained
2 stalks celery, thinly sliced
3/4 C. mayonnaise
2 T. chopped chutney
1 banana
1/2 C. salted peanuts or cashews
1/2 C. flaked coconut
1 C. (11 oz. can) mandarin oranges, drained

In large bowl, combine turkey, pineapple, celery, mayonnaise, chutney and salt; toss lightly. Cover & chill at least 2 hours. Just before serving, slice banana. Add to turkey mixture, along with nuts. Serve in lettuce cups; garnish with coconut and oranges. Makes 4 to 6 servings.

TURKEY TETRAZZINI

1 8-oz. pkg. linguini
butter or margarine
1 small onion, diced
1/4 C. flour
2 3/4 C. milk
1-2 1/2 oz. jar sliced mushrooms
1 T. chicken-flavor bouillon granules
1/2 t. salt
1/4 t. cracked pepper
1/4 C. grated Parmesan cheese
4 slices white bread
2 C. cubed cooked turkey

In 6 quart saucepot, cook linguini as label directs; drain. Return linguini to saucepot; keep warm.
Meanwhile, in 2 quart saucepan, over medium heat, in 3 T. hot butter, cook onion until tender, stirring occasionally. Stir in flour until blended. Gradually stir in milk until smooth. Then add mushrooms with their liquid, bouillon, salt, and pepper; cook, stirring constantly, until mixture is slightly thickened. Remove saucepan from heat; stir in cheese.
Tear bread into small pieces to make 2 cups coarse bread crumbs. In small saucepan over low heat, melt 3 T. butter; remove from heat, stir in bread crumbs; set aside.
Preheat oven to 350°. To linguini in saucepot, add sauce mixture & turkey; gently toss to mix well. Spoon mixture into 12" by 8" baking dish; top with bread crumbs. Bake about 20 minutes, or until heated through & bubbling. Makes 6 servings.

TURKEY A LA KING

1 small can mushrooms, reserve liquid
1/2 C. diced green pepper
1/2 C. butter
1/2 C. flour
1 t. salt
1/4 t. pepper
2 C. light cream or half & half
1 1/2 C. chicken broth
2 C. cubed cooked turkey
1 4-oz. jar pimiento, chopped
Slices of toast

In skillet, cook & stir mushrooms & green pepper in butter about 5 minutes. Blend in flour, salt, pepper. Cook on low heat, stirring until mixture is bubbly, Remove from heat, stir in cream, broth and 1/4 C. mushroom liquid. Heat to boiling, stirring constantly. Boil & stir 1 minute. Stir in turkey and pimiento, heat through. Serve over toast. Serves 8.

TURKEY RICE SOUP

4 T. vegetable oil
4-5 cloves garlic, minced
3-4 stalks celery, sliced
1/4 C. diced red pepper
1/2 C. diced green pepper
2 large & 2 small tomatoes, blanched, peeled & diced
6 large stalks asparagus, sliced in 1" pieces
1/2 C. regular white rice
2 C. diced turkey
46 oz. can College Inn Chicken Broth*
1 t. salt
1/2 t. pepper
1/4 t. dried summer savory
pinch lemon pepper
1/4 t. dried parsley
4 1/2 oz. jar sliced mushrooms

In heavy saucepan, heat oil. Add vegetables (except tomato) &
saute until tender, but not brown - 5 to 8 minutes. Add tomatoes &
saute 2 minutes. Stir in broth, seasonings & rice. Bring to boil,
stirring occasionally; reduce heat. Cover & simmer 15 minutes.
Add turkey & mushrooms; cook 5 minutes more.
*Add 2 13-3/4 oz. cans at same time, if you like more broth.

GIFTS FROM THE KITCHEN BROADCAST
JEWELED FRUIT SAUCE

1/3 C. butter

2 T. cornstarch

1/2 t. cinnamon

1/4 C. sugar

1 C. water

1/2 C. orange juice

1/2 C. candied red & green
    cherries, quartered

1/2 C. golden raisins

1 t. brandy extract

In 2 qt. saucepan, melt butter. Stir in cornstarch & cinnamon until dissolved. Add sugar, water & orange juice. Cook over medium heat, stirring occasionally, until thickened (5 to 6 min.). Stir in remaining ingredients. Serve warm over ice cream or slices of pound cake. Makes 2 1/2 C. sauce.

CREAM FUDGE

2 C. sugar

Pinch of salt

1 C. milk (scant)

2 T. cocoa (scant)

1 T. corn syrup

Boil slowly, stirring until sugar is dissolved; then occasionally to keep from sticking. Add 1 t. vanilla. Beat until thick enough. Pour onto buttered plate, let cool, cut into pieces.

POPCORN BALLS

1 C. sugar

1/3 C. corn syrup

1/3 C. water

3 qts. popcorn

1/4 C. butter

1/2 t. salt

1/2 t. vanilla

Boil first 6 ingredients until they reach the "thread" stage -- about 260°. on candy thermometer. Spread popped corn onto cookie sheets. Drizzle cooked mixture evenly over popcorn. Form quickly into balls.

163.

CANDIED PINEAPPLE RINGS

3 C. sugar   1/3 C. light corn syrup
2 cans (20 oz. size) sliced pineapple in syrup

Combine 2 cups sugar, corn syrup and 1 cup water in large, heavy
skillet; cook over medium heat, stirring constantly, until sugar is
dissolved. Continue cooking, without stirring, to 232° on candy
thermometer, or until a little dropped from spoon spins a 2-inch
thread.
Meanwhile, drain pineapple very well on paper towels. Drop 6 or 7
rings at a time into syrup; simmer slowly 5 minutes. Turn; then
simmer until translucent - about 7 more minutes. Drain on wire
rack, placed over waxed-paper-lined tray. Continue until all
pineapple is candied.
Let pineapple stand, uncovered, 24 hours. Sprinkle all sides with
1/2 C. sugar. Let stand 24 hours longer; then sprinkle with rest of
sugar. Refrigerate, covered. Keeps about two weeks. Makes 20
rings, or about 2 pounds.

BANBURY TARTS

1 1/2 pkgs. piecrust mix   1 egg yolk
1 C. prepared mincemeat (in jar)   1 T. water
3/4 C. grated sharp cheddar cheese

Prepare piecrust mix as directed on package; roll out thin on lightly floured board or pastry cloth to about 16" x 16". Cut into 12 four-inch squares. Place an equal amount of mincemeat on each square. Top mincemeat with 1 T. grated cheese. Fold each square to make a triangle; press edges together with floured tines of fork. Cut small slits in top of each. Beat egg yolk & water until well blended; brush over tarts. Place on cookie sheets. Bake at 425° for 10 to 12 minutes, or until golden brown. Serve hot or cold. Makes 12. These can also be made half size (starting with two-inch squares).

ORANGE NUT CAKES

1 C. (2 sticks) margarine, softened
2 C. sugar
4 eggs
1 1/2 C. sour cream
2 T. grated orange peel

4 C. flour
2 t. baking soda
2 t. salt
2 C. chopped walnuts

In a large mixer bowl. combine margarine, sugar, eggs & sour cream. Beat on medium speed until mixture is smooth. Blend in orange peel. Thoroughly mix flour, baking soda & salt. Stir into sour cream mixture. Mix in walnuts. (Batter will be very thick). Turn mixture into two greased 8 1/2 x 4 1/2 x 2 1/2 in. loaf pans. Spread batter evenly to edges of pans.
Bake at 350° about 1 hour and 10 minutes, or until cakes test done. Cool in pans 10 minutes. Remove from pans & finish cooling on wire racks. Frost with orange-cream glaze when cool and decorate as desired. Makes 2 cakes.

Orange-Cream Glaze: Combine 1/2 C. sour cream, 1 t. grated orange peel and 2 C. unsifted confectioners sugar. Mix until smooth.

FESTIVE RICE

Makes four 1 1/3 C. jars

4 C. long-grain rice
1/2 C. dried apricot, finely chopped
1/2 C. walnuts, finely chopped
1/4 t. ground black pepper
1/4 t. ground nutmeg
2 T. instant chicken broth granules
1/2 C. golden raisins
1 t. dried orange peel
1/4 t. ground cinnamon

In large bowl, combine all ingredients & mix well. Divide into four attractive jars. Seal and label.
Attach the following directions for cooking the rice with your gift:

In heavy 2-quart saucepan, heat 2 t. vegetable oil and 1 t. butter over medium-low heat. Add 1 medium-size onion, finely chopped; saute over medium heat until softened and just golden brown - 2 to 5 minutes. Add 1 jar of Festive Rice and stir to coat with oil. Add 1 3/4 C. water. Heat mixture to boiling over high heat, stirring occasionally. Reduce heat to low; cover with tight-fitting lid. Simmer 15 to 20 minutes. Without uncovering, remove pot from heat and set aside in warm area 10 minutes; fluff rice with fork before serving. Enjoy!

MEATLESS PASTA SAUCE

2 T. olive oil
2/3 C. (6 oz. can) Italian style tomato paste
1 medium onion, diced
3/4 C. warm water
1 T. chopped garlic
1/2 t. salt
1 small sliced zucchini
1/8 t. pepper
1 med. sliced yellow squash
1/2 t. each: dried basil & oregano
1 C. green & red bell pepper strips
Pasta of your choice
1 3/4 C. (14.5 oz) recipe ready or Italian style tomatoes, drained
        (juice reserved)
Canned sliced mushrooms (optional)
Sliced ripe olives (optional)

In medium skillet, heat oil; saute onion & garlic for 1 minute. Add
zucchini, yellow squash and bell peppers; saute for 3 to 4 minutes.
Stir in reserved tomato juice, Italian paste, water, salt & pepper &
mushrooms; simmer for 5 to 8 minutes or until vegetables are
tender. Stir in tomatoes & basil & oregano; simmer for 1 minute.
Serve sauce over prepared pasta; garnish with olives. Makes 6
servings.

SKILLET MACARONI AND CHEESE

8 oz. (approx. 2 C.) ziti or elbow macaroni
8 oz. reduced fat sharp Cheddar cheese, shredded
2 T. butter or margarine
4 oz. cooked ham, sliced & diced
2 T. flour
1/2 t. dry mustard
1 2-oz. jar diced pimento
dash pepper
1 t. dried parsley
1 3/4 C. milk

About 25 minutes before serving: Cook ziti or macaroni as label directs.

Meanwhile, in 12-inch skillet over med. heat, melt butter or margarine; whisk in flour, mustard & pepper until blended; cook 1 minute. Gradually stir in milk; cook, stirring constantly, until thickened & smooth. Remove skillet from heat; stir in cheese until melted.
Drain macaroni; stir into cheese sauce in skillet with ham, pimento, and parsley. Over low heat, heat through.   Makes 4 main-dish servings

LINGUINE AND SHRIMP

1/2 # linguine, uncooked
1 clove garlic, minced
1/2 C. Italian dressing (we use our homemade recipe)
1/4 C. chopped parsley
1/2 # small shrimp, shelled, deveined
2 t. grated lemon peel
1 each: med. yellow squash, zucchini & carrot, julienne cut
1 t. salt; dash cayenne pepper
3 green onions, cut in strips

Prepare linguine as package directs. In medium skillet, heat Italian dressing. Add remaining ingredients, except linguine. Cook & stir 8-10 minutes. Drain linguine; add to skillet, toss & serve.
Serves 4-6

PACIFIC CHICKEN BAKE

1 T. margarine
2 medium bananas, sliced
4 skinless, boneless chicken breast halves
1 can (8 oz.) crushed pineapple
3 C. (4 medium) yams, sliced
1/4 C. chopped pecans
1 C. (or more) bottled sweet & sour sauce

Steam peeled, sliced yams (about 5 - 7 min.). Melt marg. in skillet & brown chicken on both sides. In 1 1/2 qt. shallow baking dish, combine sweet potatoes, bananas, pineapple, nuts & sauce. Top w/chicken breasts. Pour more sauce over chicken. Cover w/foil & bake at 375° for 20 min, until chicken is done. Serves 4

*POPPY SEED CITRUS BREAD

recipe responsible for BREAKFAST AT THE OUTBACK

Bread:
2 C. flour
1 C. granulated sugar
1 t. baking powder
2 eggs
1/2 t. baking soda
Grated peel of 2 large lemons & 1 large orange
1/2 t. salt
1/2 t. nutmeg
1 C. sour cream
8 T. margarine, room temperature
1/4 C. poppy seeds
Glaze:
1 T. lemon juice, 1 T. orange juice,   1/4 C. powdered sugar

To prepare the bread: Sift together the flour, baking powder, soda, salt & nutmeg. With an electric mixer, cream together the margarine and granulated sugar until light. Add the eggs, one at a time, beating well after each addition. Beat in the lemon and orange peels. Slowly add the flour mixture, alternating with the sour cream. Beat to blend. Beat in the poppy seeds.
Transfer the batter to a greased & floured 9 by 5 inch loaf pan. Bake in a preheated 350° oven about one hour, or until a tester inserted in the bread comes out clean. The bread may need an additional 5-10 minutes. Let the bread cool in the pan 10 minutes before turning out onto a rack.
To prepare the glaze: Whisk together the lemon & orange juices & the powdered sugar. Brush over the warm bread. Cool completely before slicing. Or wrap and freeze after the bread has cooled.
Makes 1 loaf.

CORNMEAL-OATMEAL MUFFINS

1 C. flour
1 C. buttermilk
1 t. baking powder
1 egg
3/4 t. salt
1/3 C. packed light brown sugar
1/2 t. baking soda
1/2 C. margarine or butter, melted
1/2 C. each: yellow cornmeal & old-fashioned oats

Mix well: flour, baking powder, salt & baking soda; set aside. In medium bowl, whisk together cornmeal, & oats; mix in buttermilk. Add egg, sugar & margarine. Beat with wooden spoon until well blended. Add flour mixture; stir just until blended. Spoon into 12 greased 2 1/2 in. muffin cups. (Batter will be rather drippy.) Bake in preheated 400° oven for about 20-23 min., or until rich golden brown.

Note: I never buy buttermilk because we wind up throwing the remainder out. Instead, put 1 T. vinegar in measuring cup, fill it to the 1 C. mark w/milk, let sit while preparing first part of recipe and all will be well. Makes 12

ENGLISH MUFFIN LOAVES

5 1/2-6 C. flour
2 pkgs. dry yeast (2 T.)
1 T. sugar
2 t. salt
1/4 t. baking soda
2 C. milk
1/2 C. water
Cornmeal

Combine 3 C. flour, yeast, sugar, salt & soda. Heat liquids until very warm (120-130 deg.). Add to dry mixture, beat well, stir in enough more flour to make a stiff batter. Spoon into two 8 1/2x 41/2" pans that have been greased & sprinkled w/cornmeal. Sprinkle tops w/cornmeal. Cover; let rise in warm place for 45 min. Bake at 400° for 25 min. Remove from pans immediately & cool. To serve: Slice & toast. Makes about 16 slices per loaf. Makes 2 loaves.

FALL PEAR-CRANBERRY CONSERVE

6 1/2 C. sugar
1 C. cranberries
1 C. water
1 1/2 - 2# pears, cored, peeled & finely chopped (3 C.)
3/4 C. finely chopped pecans
2 T. finely shredded lemon peel
1 6 oz. pkg. liquid fruit pectin (2 foil pouches)
1/3 C. lemon juice

In 3 qt. saucepan combine sugar, cranberries & water. Bring to boil, stirring frequently, till sugar is dissolved. Remove from heat. Add chopped pears, nuts & lemon peel. Let stand 10 min., stirring occasionally. Combine pectin & lemon juice; add to pear mixture. Stir for 3 min. Ladle at once into clean jars, leaving 1/2". Seal. Let stand several hours. or till set. Store up to 3 weeks in frig. or 1 year. in freezer. Thaw in refrig. before serving

LEMON CRUMB MUFFINS

<u>Topping:</u> 1 1/2 C. cake flour   1 1/2 C. sugar
                4 T. melted butter
Make a streusel topping by sifting together the cake flour & sugar.
Drizzle in enough melted butter to make crumbs the consistency of
cornmeal. Set aside. (This makes enough for two or more
recipes.)

1/2 t. salt
1/2 t. baking soda
3 C. sugar
4 1/2 C. flour
1 1/2 C. butter
6 eggs
11/2 C. sour cream
2 T., plus 2 t. fresh lemon juice
granted rind of 4 lemons
3/4 C. sugar
1/3 C. fresh lemon juice

In a large bowl, sift together salt, baking soda, 3 C. of sugar and 4
1/2 C. flour. Add butter and blend with a fork until mixture looks
like coarse crumbs. In another bowl, beat eggs, then add sour
cream, lemon juice and rind. Add to flour mixture and mix.

Spray muffin tins with Pam (or line with paper muffin cups), then
fill each tin 3/4 full. Cover with streusel topping, and bake at 350°
for 20 to 25 minutes. Remove from oven and allow to cool.

Prepare glaze by mixing 1/3 C. of lemon juice and 3/4 C. of sugar.
With a toothpick, punch 6 to 8 holes around crown of each muffin;
generously spoon glaze over the top. Makes 2 1/2 dozen.

175.

CHEDDAR CORNMEAL MUFFINS

1 C. all-purpose flour
3/4 C. yellow cornmeal
1/4 C. sugar
1/2 t. baking soda
1/4 t. salt
1 C. (4 oz.) grated Chedarella Cheese (Land O Lakes)
1/2 C. butter, melted
1 C. sour cream
1 egg, slightly beaten

Heat oven to 375°. In large bowl combine flour, cornmeal, sugar,
baking soda & salt. In medium bowl, combine all remaining
ingredients. Stir in flour mixture just until moistened. Batter will
be stiff.   Spoon into greased 12 cup muffin pan. Bake for 18 to 23
minutes, or until light golden brown. (Makes 1 dozen) Can also be
prepared in greased 9 in square baking pan. Bake for 25 to 35
minutes.

SAVORY POT (OR OVEN) ROAST

Seasoned flour: 1 C. flour
                 1/2 t. ea.: garlic, celery & onion salt
                 1 t. salt
                 1/4 t. pepper
                 1 t. paprika
2 - 3 T. salad oil
3 - 4 lbs. beef rump roast
Pinch of nutmeg
2 - 4 large onions, sliced
2 cans College Inn Beef Broth
4 T. tomato paste
3 T. brown sugar
1 t. paprika
3 T. vinegar - or 1/4 C. red wine

Mix seasoned flour, use as much as needed to coat roast. Save rest in double brown bag to use with other meat, chicken etc. (Small cuts of meat can be dropped in bag, bag closed & shaken, to easily coat.) Add a pinch of nutmeg to coating for roast. Heat oil in heavy pan, brown the meat on all sides, then remove. Brown onions lightly in pan. Replace meat, add remaining ingredients (which have been whisked together in a bowl). Cover, cook over medium heat until it comes to a boil. Then reduce heat, making sure it continues to boil gently. Turn meat from time to time, so no side dries out. A 4# roast will take about 3 1/2 hrs. to cook. If preferred, bake in oven at 350° for 2 1/2 to 3 hrs. Scrub & peel center section of small red potatoes or peel & halve regular potatoes & add to roast for last hour of cooking. At beginning of last half hour, add peeled & sectioned carrots. Serve with pan juices. Makes about 10 servings. This freezes well, too.

CITRUS SWEET POTATOES

2 large yams (orange)
6 T. butter, melted
1 lemon, washed
2 oranges, washed
6 T. brown sugar
2 C. orange juice
1/2 t. vanilla
1/2 t. ea.: cinnamon & nutmeg

Peel potatoes & cut into 1/4 inch slices. Place in a 8 or 9 inch square baking pan. Slice lemon and oranges very thinly and place these slices on top of sweet potatoes. Combine melted butter, sugar, orange juice, cinnamon and nutmeg. Stir in vanilla. Pour mixture over sweet potato mixture, cover with plastic wrap & let stand 1 hour.

Bake, uncovered, at 350° for 1 and 1/4 hours, basting often with pan juices, or until potatoes are tender in juice. Serves 4

SOUTHWESTERN CORN & PEPPER GRATIN

1 T. olive oil
2 3/4 C. fresh corn kernels (about 4 ears) divided
1 C. chopped onion
1 C. each, diced green & red pepper
2 T. minced seeded jalapeno pepper
3/4 t. salt, divided
1/2 t. ground cumin
1/2 t. freshly ground pepper
1/4 C. (1 oz.) shredded sharp cheddar cheese
3/4 C. skim milk
1/4 C. nonfat dry milk
3 eggs
1 T. flour

Preheat oven to 425°. Heat oil in a large non-stick skillet over
medium heat. Add onions; saute 5 min. or until tender. Add
peppers, 1/4 t. salt & the pepper; saute 5 min. Add 2 C. corn, the
jalapeno and cumin; saute 5 min. or until peppers are crisp-tender.
Remove from heat & stir in cheese. Spoon mixture into a 2-quart
baking dish which has been coated w/cooking spray.
Combine 3/4 C. corn, 1/2 t. salt, skim & dry milks, flour & eggs in
a blender; process until smooth. Pour over vegetables. Bake for 35
minutes or until golden. Makes 4 servings.

CRANBERRY HASH

4 medium-size turnips, peeled & chopped
2 C. cranberries
4 medium-size carrots, peeled & cut in rounds
1/2 C. sugar
2 T. butter or margarine
2 medium-size apples, cored, peeled, & chopped
2 T. lemon juice
1 t. salt

Heat oven to 350°. In 3-quart casserole, combine all ingredients. Cover casserole tightly & bake 40 to 45 minutes or until vegetables are tender. Stir before serving. Serve hot. Makes 10 servings

TARTAR SAUCE

1 C. mayonnaise
2 T. minced dill pickle
2 t. cut up pimento
1 tsp. grated onion
1 T. minced parsley

Combine all ingredients & mix well. Best if prepared several hours ahead. Chill. Makes 1 cup

COCKTAIL SAUCE

1/2 C. chili sauce
2 t. lemon juice
dash of Tabasco sauce
1 T. prepared horseradish
1 t. Worcestershire sauce

Combine all ingredients. Mix well. & chill. Makes approx. 2/3 cup.

BOB'S BAKED SALMON (for two)

Marinate 2 six oz. salmon fillets for two hours. Pour off marinade and bake, skin side down, in a pre-heated oven at 425° for 15-17 minutes.

Salmon will flake easily when ready. Serve on warmed plates.

Marinade
1/2 cup dry white wine
1/4 cup olive oil
3 cloves garlic, minced
2 T. Krazy Mixed Up Pepper
1/2 T. sea or kosher salt

BOB'S BROILED SEA SCALLOPS (for two)

10 large sea scallops thoroughly washed in cold water
1/2 bottle/can of your favorite beer.
1/2 - (4 T). stick of butter, melted - do not brown
6 large sprigs of fresh parsley, chopped
4 cloves garlic, minced
 Dry bread crumbs

Combine parsley & garlic in melted butter. Keep mixture at low heat. Wash scallops and marinate in bowl with 1/2 can of beer for 30 minutes. (You can drink the rest as you work.)

Roll scallops in bread crumbs and place on cookie sheet/pizza pan. Stir butter mixture and evenly drizzle over scallops.

Broil for 3-4 minutes or until bread crumbs brown.
Serve on warmed plates.

SPICED CRANBERRY MOLD

1 can (20 oz.) crushed pineapple in juice
1 can (11 oz.) mandarin oranges
1 stick cinnamon
4 whole cloves
1/2 t. coriander seeds
1 pkg. (6 oz.) cranberry jello
1 C. ruby port wine
1 C. broken pecans
1 can (1#) whole-berry cranberry sauce

Drain pineapple & oranges, reserving juices. Place juices in measuring cup & add water to make 2 cups. Add cinnamon stick, cloves & coriander seeds to juices & bring to a boil. Remove from heat and let stand 20 minutes.

Place dry gelatin in mixing bowl. Return juice mixture to boil. Strain & add to gelatin. Stir to dissolve. Add port. Chill until mixture is thickened slightly, about the consistency of egg whites. Stir in drained fruits, pecans and cranberry sauce, mixing thoroughly. Pour into 7-cup mold or large glass baking dish and chill several hours or overnight.

To serve, unmold gelatin onto serving plate (if using mold) & garnish with greens. Or serve individual portions on lettuce leaves. Makes about 8 to 10 servings.

SUMMER FRUIT COMPOTE IN LIME SYRUP

1 1/2 C. sugar
1 C. water
1/4 t. grated lime peel
1/4 C. lime juice
1 1/2 C. each, green seedless grapes & blueberries
3 plums, diced
3 nectarines, diced

In large saucepan, stir sugar & water over low heat until sugar dissolves. Bring to boil, reduce heat, cover & simmer 5 minutes. Remove from heat; stir in peel & juice. Cool. Add fruits; toss gently. Cover & chill several hours or overnight. Makes 8 servings. Very nice over ice cream, frozen yogurt or pound cake.

SOUR CREAM POUND CAKE

3 C. flour
1/4 t. baking soda
1/4 t. salt
3 C. sugar
1/2 lb. butter

6 eggs
1 C. sour cream
1 t. vanilla extract
Confectioners sugar

Sift together flour, baking soda, salt. Using electric mixer, cream together sugar & butter until fluffy & light. Add eggs, one at a time, beating after each addition. Stir in sour cream & vanilla. Gradually mix dry ingredients into egg mixture until completely blended. Turn into greased & floured 10-inch tube pan. Bake at 350° one hour & 25 minutes, or until toothpick inserted comes out clean. Remove from pan, cool on rack. Before serving, sprinkle with confectioners sugar.

CRANBERRY APPLE PIE

Pastry for 9 inch two crust pie
3/4 C. brown sugar
1/4 C. sugar
1/3 C. flour
1 t. cinnamon
4 C. pared, sliced, tart apples
2 C. fresh or frozen cranberries
2 T. butter

Preheat oven to 425°. In large bowl, combine sugars, flour & cinnamon. Add fruit; mix well. Turn into pastry-lined pan. Dot with butter. Cover & cut slits in top crust. Seal edges. Bake 40 minutes, or until golden brown.

PUMPKIN-SPICE CAKE

1 C. corn oil

4 large eggs

2 t. vanilla

3 T. orange juice

2 C. pumpkin puree

3 C. flour

2 C. sugar

1/2 t. salt

1 T. baking soda

2 t. ground cinnamon

1/2 t. ground allspice

1/4. t. ground mace

1/2 t. ground nutmeg

2 t. ground ginger

1 C. chopped pecans

Ginger Cream Cheese Frosting:

8 oz. cream cheese, softened

3 1/2 C. confectioners sugar

2 T. finely chopped crystallized ginger

6 T. butter, softened

1 T. lemon juice

In a large bowl, combine the oil, eggs, vanilla, orange juice, and pumpkin. Beat well. Place the flour, sugar, salt, baking soda, cinnamon, allspice, mace, nutmeg & ginger in another large bowl and whisk to blend. Fold the flour mixture slowly into the pumpkin mixture until well incorporated. Stir in the pecans. Divide the batter between 2 greased & floured 9-inch round cake pans. Bake at 350° for about 45 minutes, until the layers test done. Cool in the pans on wire racks. Turn out and frost when completely cool.

To make the frosting, beat the cream cheese & butter. Sift in the confectioners sugar & whip until fluffy. Stir in the lemon juice & fold in the crystallized ginger. Sandwich the two layers with a thin coating of frosting, then frost the sides and top of the cake.

ESPRESSO FROZEN DESSERT

2/3 C. finely ground espresso coffee
3 C. boiling water
1 C. sugar
1 (2 in. x 1/2 in.) strip lemon zest
1 C. very cold whipping cream
Unsweetened cocoa powder

Place ground coffee in coffee filter and holder set over 1-quart measure. Slowly pour boiling water over coffee. Stir sugar into hot liquid until dissolved. Twist lemon zest and add to coffee. Refrigerate until very cold or overnight.

When cold, remove lemon zest and discard. Pour cold coffee into 8 or 9 in. square metal pan and put in freezer until edges begin to set, about 1 hour. Using fork, break up and stir frozen edges into soft center and return to freezer. Repeat freezing and stirring until espresso is evenly semi-frozen but not solid. Serve at this point or beat with fork and transfer to plastic container. Keep frozen until just before serving.

When ready to serve, whip cream until stiff peaks form. Spoon frozen espresso into large goblets. Top each with whipped cream and sprinkle with a little cocoa powder run through a sieve. Makes 4 servings.

CHOCOLATE CAKE WITH WHITE FROSTING

2 C. sugar	2 eggs
1 3/4 C. flour	1 C. buttermilk
3/4 C. cocoa	1/2 C. vegetable oil
1 t. baking powder	1 t. vanilla
1 t. salt	1 C. strong black coffee

Combine dry ingredients in a large bowl. In a separate bowl, mix together eggs, buttermilk, oil & vanilla, then add to dry ingredients and mix well, scraping bowl. Add coffee, mix well & scrape bowl. Beat for 2 minutes on medium speed. Batter will be thin.
Pour into two 9 inch cake pans, which have been lined with waxed paper in the bottom and greased. Bake at 350° for 35 to 45 minutes. Test with toothpick to determine when done; cover pans loosely with foil if cake browns too quickly. Cool cakes for 10 minutes, then remove from pans.

Icing:
2 sticks margarine, softened
2 8-oz. packages cream cheese, softened
2 t. vanilla
7 C. powdered sugar

Cream together margarine & cream cheese, then add vanilla & powdered sugar. To ice, carefully slice cake layers in half (to make 4 layers), fill and frost.

ABOUT THE BELFANCES

Bob began his career as a professional radio actor at the age of nine. Since then, Bob has directed over 200 plays and musicals, written and directed award- winning documentary films for Omnibus Film Productions, a company in which he was part owner, and owned and operated the Priscilla Beach Summer Theater. In New York, Lee Strasberg invited Bob, then a fledgling director, to observe the work at the famous Actors Studio. Bob worked with and/or directed Alfred Drake, Ruth Chatterton, Howard da Silva, Alan Alda and his late father Robert, Ray Wise, Paul Dooley and many other well-known professionals.

Bob was the first resident professional Artistic & Managing Director of the Weathervane Community Playhouse. He was responsible for transforming this organization into one of Ohio's leading non-professional theaters and moving the organization into a new and much larger theater complex.

Bob, along with a host of dedicated volunteers, helped to save the old Loews Movie Theater, now the Akron Civic Theater, from the wrecker's ball. This theater is one of only a handful of the "movie palaces" still extant.

He has also served as a consultant for theaters and educational facilities, recently wrote, produced and directed a musical revue *DIVAS DAMES AND DOLLS* and, with wife Carol, has been seen and heard on radio spots all over the U.S.

Carol's route to professional theater, radio and television was more circuitous. Performing on stages from the age of four, she always felt comfortable there. When people "drafted" her into high school, college and community theater, she was a willing participant.

Armed with a B.S. in Home Economics from the University of Akron ("They told me Math was no field for a woman!"), she climbed the corporate ladder at Firestone Tire & Rubber Co. One promotion away from the executive wing, she realized that theater was still the dominant love of her life.

Back to graduate school for an M.A. in Speech/Theatre at the University of Akron and a part-time faculty position. Already quite active in radio commercials, selling products "on air" helped supplement her income while in grad school and beyond. She taught Speech, Theatre and Communication Dept. classes at U. of A. and theatre classes at Cuyahoga Community College (near Cleveland). Being asked to teach non-credit, evening acting classes for adults at U. of A. eventually led her to form adult acting classes at Weathervane Community Playhouse and, with Bob, to teach acting for the Older Adult Service and Information System.

She also found time to tour with the late Paul Lynde and Alice Ghostly; perform with Arlene Dahl; work as casting director and performer on two award-winning national radio series, "An American Idea" and (with Bob) "America 2000"; continue doing commercials, voice-overs and narration for radio, TV, industrials and training films, and co-produce (with Bob) Murder Mystery Weekends at various locations in Northeast Ohio.

CENTERFOLD PHOTOGRAPHY

Court House, Herald Building, Brenda de la Mora, John Barnes courtesy of The Morgan County Herald.